the
minimalist
entrepreneur

the minimalist entrepreneur

HOW GREAT FOUNDERS DO MORE WITH LESS

Sahil Lavingia

PORTFOLIO · PENGUIN

Portfolio / Penguin
An imprint of Penguin Random House LLC
penguinrandomhouse.com

Most Portfolio books are available at a discount when purchased in quantity for
sales promotions or corporate use. Special editions, which include personalized
covers, excerpts, and corporate imprints, can be created when purchased in large
quantities. For more information, please call (212) 572-2232 or e-mail
specialmarkets@penguinrandomhouse.com. Your local bookstore can also assist
with discounted bulk purchases using the Penguin Random House corporate
Business-to-Business program. For assistance in locating a participating retailer,
e-mail B2B@penguinrandomhouse.com.

Library of Congress Cataloging-in-Publication Data

Names: Lavingia, Sahil, author.
Title: The minimalist entrepreneur : how great founders
do more with less / Sahil Lavingia.
Description: New York : Portfolio/Penguin, [2021] | Includes
bibliographical references and index.
Identifiers: LCCN 2021012336 (print) | LCCN 2021012337 (ebook) |
ISBN 9780593192399 (hardcover) | ISBN 9780593192405 (ebook)
Subjects: LCSH: New business enterprises.
Classification: LCC HD62.5 .L389 2021 (print) | LCC HD62.5 (ebook) |
DDC 658.1/1—dc23
LC record available at https://lccn.loc.gov/2021012336
LC ebook record available at https://lccn.loc.gov/2021012337

International edition ISBN: 9780593421338

Printed in the United States of America
2nd Printing

Interior illustrations by Brian Box Brown

Book design by Chris Welch

contents

INTRODUCTION

I started my career chasing unicorns. I joined Pinterest as employee number two, but in 2011, I left before my stock vested to build my own billion-dollar company.

I had spent a weekend building the prototype of Gumroad, a tool that helped creators sell their products online. No complicated setup. No elaborate storefront. Just a link for customers to pay and you're in business. More than fifty thousand people visited the site on the first day, and I was sure I was on the cusp of something big.

The first step: raising money from VCs. As a nineteen-year-old solo founder, I found myself walking up and down the mythical Sand Hill Road, sweating through my jeans, having meetings in the same rooms where the decisions to fund companies like Netflix, Apple, Amazon, Facebook, and Google had happened. I ended up raising more than $8 million in venture capital from renowned Silicon Valley investors, including Accel Partners (early investor in Facebook), Kleiner Perkins (early investor in Google, Amazon, and Apple), Max Levchin (cofounder of PayPal), Naval Ravikant (cofounder of AngelList), and Chris Sacca (early investor in Twitter, Square, and Uber). They too thought they saw a unicorn galloping in the distance.

The chase was on. In short order, I built a world-class team—recruiting talent out of companies like Stripe, Yelp, and Amazon—and together we went to work on building a world-class product. I was confident that I'd soon be strolling through Allen & Company's annual Sun Valley conference, strategizing about the fight against malaria arm-in-arm with Bill Gates and Warren Buffett. I was never in it for the money, I told myself. I wanted to make an impact, but quietly. When I became a tech titan, I was going to be the kind of titan magazine profiles called "down-to-earth."

I didn't make it to Sun Valley that summer. Or the summer after that. The closest I ever got to Bill Gates was watching him speak at a Kleiner Perkins CEO summit. Gumroad's pitched flight into the stratosphere leveled off after we burned through about $10 million in venture capital. After nine months of trying to raise more funding, we failed. In October 2015, I laid off three-quarters of the staff—including many good friends.

Once the bleeding stopped, it was time to reassess. Gumroad was still operational, but I felt like a complete failure. With many in my circle still focused on raising money, hiring employees, and chasing their own billion-dollar companies—some successfully—I couldn't bear to stick around Silicon Valley. For much of 2016, I kept my apartment in San Francisco but spent most of my time traveling and writing fiction, convinced that even if I couldn't hack it in Startupland, I could still build a life for myself as a digital nomad. While I was inspired by Tim Ferriss's *The 4-Hour Workweek*, it didn't take long to realize that operating Gumroad as a lifestyle business wasn't for me. I was still trying to figure out what came next when I saw a tweet from Brandon Sanderson, one of my favorite authors, about a science-fiction and fantasy writing class he was teaching in Provo, Utah. In January 2017, I jumped on the opportunity to save rent and save face by moving to a place where no one knew me. There, I could figure out how to regroup even as I kept Gumroad afloat.

I knew things would be very different in Provo, but the contrast still surprised me. In San Francisco, being successful means you've made a lot of money (which, in San Francisco, is a *lot* of money). In Utah, it means you're married and active in the church. My new Provo friends told me that I'd been crazy trying to build a billion-dollar company in the first place. Why wasn't Gumroad good enough as it was? After all, I had a sustainable business serving a group of customers I loved. What more could I want?

At first, I couldn't quite grasp what they were talking about, but after living in Provo for a couple of years away from the white-hot epicenter of venture capital, I came to agree. While the unicorn I was chasing turned out to be more of a Shetland pony, my original vision *was* being realized. Thousands of creators were using Gumroad to build their own creative businesses. Real people in the real world were paying their mortgages or topping off their kids' college funds or simply paying for a few extra lattes by selling courses, ebooks, and software online.

Over time, I realized that the problem wasn't Gumroad, the problem was me. I was still so focused on that elusive unicorn, I couldn't see the thriving business humming along right in front of me. Gumroad was profitable, the right size for its market, and enabling more and more writers, coders, crafters, and other makers to achieve their dreams with each passing day. Gumroad may have been a crappy investment for a few venture capitalists, but it was still a great company for its customers.

In the year after the layoffs, when I worked by myself, Gumroad *still* sent approximately $40 million to our creators, without *any* content marketing or paid advertising. Just creators telling other creators. When I recommitted to growing the company again in 2019, I continued to say no to those things I had said yes to previously, and focused solely on what would create more value for our creators. (Namely, shipping a better product.) It worked: In 2020 Gumroad sent more than $140 million to our creators, up 87 percent over the year before, all while remaining profitable.

Companies like mine may not grace the covers of glossy magazines or inspire Hollywood biopics, but they drive real, positive change and empower their founders, customers, and employees alike. I know that now, but it took me years to decouple my self-worth from my net worth and to realize that I hadn't failed. I had succeeded.

In February 2019, I wrote about my experience in a *Medium* essay, "Reflecting on My Failure to Build a Billion-Dollar Company," that struck a chord with millions. Since then, I've had the chance to connect with entrepreneurs and aspiring entrepreneurs who, deep down, would much rather build a sustainable business like Gumroad than chase a unicorn. They just think it's weird and uncool to express that desire when the media and our bigger-is-better culture keeps telling them that a unicorn is the only kind of business worth creating.

While that may be the right path for some companies, for many more it's not. Yet plenty of early-stage startups still end up raising venture capital because they *can't* fund their businesses in a sustainable way through profits. As a result, they're locked into the pursuit of huge, winner-take-all markets where growth is the most important asset of their businesses, not revenues, profits, or sustainability.

To help me reconcile those differences, I asked myself certain questions over and over again: What do I actually care to change? If I could fix one thing about my corner of the world, what would that be? What kind of business do I really want to build, own, and run?

Other founders and future founders have asked themselves similar questions and come to similar realizations. Many of their stories are included in this book. I call these people "minimalist entrepreneurs," and I call their companies "minimalist businesses."

Building a minimalist business does not mean settling for second best. Instead, it's about creating sustainable companies that have the flexibility to take risks to serve the greater good, all while empowering others to do the same. Being profitable, hopefully from the very beginning, means being able to focus and to stay focused on the reason you started a business in the first place: to help others.

Historically, entrepreneurs have played a crucial role in driving technological and social progress. This is even more necessary today, when big corporations are required by law to prioritize shareholder value over, among other things, actual value. In researching this book, I've found countless examples of businesses such as Basecamp, Wistia, Missouri Star Quilt Company, and many other honest-to-goodness, highly scalable companies incredibly focused on solving meaningful problems with beautiful products, services, and software that people love—and making a profit doing it. Each company goes about things their own way depending on the specific community they're building for, but they all focus on problem-solving and not taking themselves too seriously. No matter their differences, we can learn from them all.

Unfortunately, the word "entrepreneur" has a weird taint to it. I remember going to a "Career Fair" at school and not identifying with the "entrepreneurs" at all. They seemed like businessmen (they were always men), and I didn't even like business. I liked making things! Eventually I realized that a business is not an end in and of itself. A business is a tool to make or do stuff, a legal structure; that's it. At first I didn't need a company, but eventually my creations required a legal structure, a team, and an operation to make the stuff I wanted to make, so I started a business.

When I made my transition from unicorn chaser to minimalist entrepreneur, I had to wrap my head around another new normal. This book is about deconstructing the myths we tell ourselves about the best way to build impactful businesses to change the abstract, singular "world," and about seeking the truth about how to build the businesses that will make us and our communities wealthier, healthier, and happier.

In the end, my failure to launch Gumroad into the stratosphere was the best thing that ever happened to me, because it taught me the very real consequences behind a "growth at all costs" mindset. Unfortunately, it took me eight years, and

a lot of pain, to realize it. I hope this book will help other aspiring entrepreneurs learn the lessons I learned without the
painful layoffs and years of soul-searching. The overwhelming response to the viral essay I wrote about my experience
is more proof that this promise resonates with many.

This book, part manifesto, part manual, will help you design, build, and successfully grow your own right-size business. Read it again and again, especially when you feel stuck.
But keep in mind that you definitely do not need to *finish* this
book to *start*. Start as soon as you can. Start before you feel
ready. Start today.

You don't learn, then start. You start, then learn.

Now, let's get to it!

the
minimalist
entrepreneur

the minimalist entrepreneur

The beginnings of all things are small.

—CICERO

Atlanta-based web developer Peter Askew loves to get things off the top shelf at the supermarket for people who can't reach the same heights he can. A six-foot-eight former high school basketball star, Askew sees being helpful as the pillar of his business strategy, but it wasn't always that way. When the dot-com bubble burst in 2001 and he was laid off from eTour, a websurfing guide he helped build and grow, he had to ask himself, "Is this how I want to live? Is this how I can be of service to the world?"

He knew he could get another job thanks to his background in marketing analytics, but he was also disillusioned. Money and prestige were not nearly as important to him as independence and freedom. Eventually he wound up with another role in advertising where he was exposed to a wide range of business models as thousands of new web businesses came online, but in the evening and on weekends, he threw himself into his side projects, learning about web development, domain names, and how to monetize web traffic.

That's how he stumbled on an idea that would change his life. What if instead of buying new domain names, which often took months to rank highly in search engine results, he bought expired domain names, which already had some degree of visibility? Other people were parking ads on expired domains or flipping them, but Askew had something else in mind, the seed of an idea that was driven by the questions he had started to ask himself about his work. Rather than trying to make a quick buck, he would build real businesses around domain names, asking himself with each one, "Do I feel inspired? Is there a real business here?," and, most of all, "Can I be helpful?"

He experimented with randomly created names and ventures that didn't quite work before he realized that "the domain name always comes first, the business idea comes second." In 2009, that domain name was duderanch.com. Askew bought it and launched a directory, traveling to more than fifty dude ranches to meet the owners of the destinations he featured on his site. Eventually he partnered with the owner of guestranches.com, and the two built a curated list of destination ranches around the country. The success of that venture, which he worked on for ten years and sold in 2019, gave him the time and financial freedom to buy more domain names and develop other niche businesses. Some succeeded, others didn't.

In 2014, Askew saw that VidaliaOnions.com was up for auction. Until then, he had focused on information-based businesses, but something about the domain name appealed to him. So did the onions, frankly. As a Georgia native, he knew of Vidalias—a sweet, mild variety that some fans eat raw like an apple. The only trouble was that he didn't know anything about the onion business. Or farming in general, for that matter.

Regardless, he put down a $2,200 bid, confident that someone in the business would come in higher. (If bidding on interesting domain names like this sounds like a neat hobby, you may be a minimalist entrepreneur.) When he won the auction five minutes later, he was pleasantly surprised, but he filed it away for later and went back to work on other projects.

As the days went by, though, he couldn't stop thinking about Vidalias. "[The domain] kept nudging me," he writes in his essay "I Sell Onions on the Internet," and "after a month, I began to understand what it was telling me. That I buy pears from Harry & David every year, and I should mimic that same service for Vidalia onions. Instead of farm-to-door pears, farm-to-door Vidalia onions." He saw a way he could be helpful to others, and a new minimalist business was born.

Askew didn't eat Vidalias himself, but he knew that many people did, both from his own experience and from strong search volume for the phrase on Google Trends. But he still had his doubts. "I'm not a farmer," he worried. "I have no logistics or distribution system setup."

He got started anyway. His first step was to reach out to a trade group that put him in touch with Aries Haygood, the owner of an award-winning Vidalia farm in operation for over two decades that had, crucially, a packing shed. He used his own money to put up a new site on VidaliaOnions.com, and then, "[while] the farm concentrated on the Vidalia, I concentrated on customer service, marketing, branding, web development, & logistics," he recalled. "I didn't have other projects that were this front-facing, customer wise. And I discovered I immensely enjoyed it."

Askew and Haygood estimated fifty orders for their first season. They received more than six hundred.

It would be at this point in the life cycle of a VC-funded business that the investors would start getting frisky. "Six hundred orders when we expected fifty?" they'd exclaim. "Time to quintuple your hiring. Come to think of it, what does the international market for Vidalia onions look like? A few million in ad spending, a viral video, and we'll have Vidalias trending worldwide. We'll probably need people on the ground in London, Tokyo, and Sydney. Time to raise another round." And on it goes. Picture a little kid blowing a balloon up for the first time, until . . .

Askew himself couldn't help but consider trying to accelerate the company's growth, but he stuck to what he had learned over the years and focused instead on profitability. He knew that the previous owners of VidaliaOnions.com had gone belly up trying to sell salad dressings and relishes in addition to the onions themselves. So instead, he slowly built the business in front of him, figuring out how to sell Vidalia onions to the market of potential customers within the range of timely and affordable shipping from that one packing shed.

He made mistakes, of course. At one point, he lost thousands of dollars on faulty shipping boxes, an error that nearly shuttered the operation. But he also made small process improvements year by year, like implementing an automated shipping system rather than manually entering customer orders and printing UPS labels. A few years in, the business was profitable, growing organically at its own pace, and he was having fun.

Six years in, Askew's pet project has become a full-fledged business, which makes his many customers happy and has a positive impact in the local community. He no longer sees it as just another experiment along with all of his other cast-off domain names. VidaliaOnions.com is becoming his mission:

> Honestly, my customers would be quite upset if we disappeared. Last season, while I called a gentleman back regarding a phone order, his wife answered. While I introduced myself, she interrupted me mid-sentence and hollered in exaltation to her husband: "THE VIDALIA MAN! THE VIDALIA MAN! PICK UP THE PHONE!"
>
> At that moment, I realized we were doing something right. Something helpful. Something that was making a positive impact. . . . It's immensely gratifying. I feel so fortunate to be associated with this industry.

Maybe it's the onions, but Askew's story brings a tear to my eye. There is something profoundly beautiful in a value-oriented mission and a genuine purpose driven by your own lived experience. This is what being a minimalist entrepreneur is all about: making a difference while making a living.

The Minimalist Entrepreneur

Before I started to write this book, I wouldn't have described myself as a minimalist entrepreneur. I would have said I was a founder committed to a new kind of startup, one that prioritized profitability over growth and positive impact over moving fast and breaking things. Instead of capturing as much value as possible, I was determined to create as much value as possible for our customers and our community.

I'm not the only one. In this book, you'll meet dozens of entrepreneurs like Peter Askew and others who are taking the same approach to building their companies. In the past years, I've exchanged ideas on Twitter or at conferences with all of them, and the more people I talked to, the more I felt we should label this new pathway that uses the advent of software to democratize and normalize business creation for everyone.

Minimalist entrepreneurs are all unique, as is every path to success, but I've tried my best to coalesce my learnings into a single, repeatable playbook.

The steps to becoming a minimalist entrepreneur map to a function of the minimalist business—and, not coincidentally, to the chapters in this book. Each chapter builds on the previous one—just as addition leads to multiplication leads to algebra leads to calculus—until finally, at the end of the book, you'll be fully equipped to become a minimalist entrepreneur yourself. You can read it all the way through, but you should also feel free to hop around; everyone is at a different stage in their business-building journey.

○ **PUT PROFITABILITY FIRST**
Minimalist entrepreneurs create businesses that are profitable at all costs. Many businesses never intend to stick around long enough to be profitable. Instead, the plan is to sell the business before profits become necessary, raising money from investors along the way. Minimalist entrepreneurs aim to be profitable from day one or soon after, because profit is oxygen for businesses. And they do that by selling a product to customers, not by selling their users to advertisers.

○ **START WITH COMMUNITY**
Minimalist entrepreneurs build on a foundation of community. They don't ask "How can I help?" but are instead observant and cultivate authentic relationships. They spend

time and effort to learn and to build trust, focusing on the market part of "product-market fit" (a term coined by venture capitalist Marc Andreessen for being in a good market with a product that can satisfy that market) before they build anything at all.

○ **BUILD AS LITTLE AS POSSIBLE**

When they do build, minimalist entrepreneurs build only what they need to, automating or outsourcing the rest. Similarly, minimalist businesses do one thing and do it well. They work side by side with their customers to iterate toward a solution, and make sure it's worth paying for, before they take it to customers outside of their communities.

○ **SELL TO YOUR FIRST HUNDRED CUSTOMERS**

Minimalist entrepreneurs don't spend time convincing people—they spend time educating people. Selling is a discovery process, and minimalist entrepreneurs use sales as an opportunity to talk to potential customers one by one about their products while simultaneously educating themselves about the problem they are trying to solve for them. Selling this way is a long game built on relationships and vulnerability, not a one-day grand opening extravaganza followed by selling to strangers.

○ **MARKET BY BEING YOU**

Speaking of vulnerability, minimalist entrepreneurs share their stories, from struggle to success. The best marketing shows the world who you—and your product—really are. Minimalist entrepreneurs understand that people care about other people, and educate, inspire, and entertain whenever and wherever they can. Instead of making headlines, they make fans—who turn themselves into customers over time.

○ **GROW YOURSELF AND YOUR BUSINESS MINDFULLY**
Minimalist entrepreneurs own their businesses, they don't let their businesses own them. They don't spend money they don't have, and they don't sacrifice profitability for scale. At this point, it becomes a game to lose . . . and minimalist entrepreneurs don't lose.

○ **BUILD THE HOUSE YOU WANT TO LIVE IN**
Minimalist entrepreneurs hire other minimalist entrepreneurs. Instead of following the status quo, they build their companies from first principles, alienating almost everyone. The way you do things won't be for everyone, but it will be really great for a few people, and if you define your values early and often and tell the world who you are, they will find you. Conventional wisdom about how we work, when we work, and where we work is changing fast. Minimalist entrepreneurs understand there are few rules.

Even when you've successfully built your minimalist business, the journey isn't over. Spoiler alert: It never is. Minimalist entrepreneurs know that life is about more than just their companies. The true magic of entrepreneurship is that you and your business can improve the quality of life of many people. And it doesn't have to be millions; "enough" is what you decide it is, not a specific amount.

If you're nodding along, great. If you're still skeptical, well, that's okay too. I have 50,000 words and a few hours to convince you. Just keep reading!

Chase Profitability, Not Unicorns

Building a minimalist business is not a get-rich-quick proposition, but it *is* a get-rich-slowly one if you embrace profitability, not growth, as the key indicator of your company's success. Profitability means sustainability. Instead of treading water until a lifeboat comes along to save you—which is how many founders think about raising their next round of VC funding—it means building your own boat.

And while I do think the minimalist entrepreneur mindset leads to a near-100-percent success rate, I'm willing to concede that it may only happen over the course of many experiments. That's why profitability matters. If you're profitable, you can take *unlimited* shots on goal, virtually guaranteeing your success as long as you keep learning from your customers. Most people don't start. Most people who start don't continue. Most people who continue give up. Many winners are just the last ones standing. Don't give up.

We're moving past an era of gatekeeping, where bosses and universities and venture capitalists decide who gets to try and who doesn't. Information about how to start and scale companies is now available to founders around the world, and it's cheaper too, which means there are fewer and fewer reasons to raise money from venture capitalists. There's nothing inherently wrong with raising money, and not all unicorns are evil. I raised money for Gumroad (and, as you'll read later, have again, but in a very different way), and there are companies like Pinterest, Lyft, Slack, and others that raised venture capital, grew quickly, yet stayed focused on their customers. But much of the venture capital model depends on creating unsustainable growth and destroying successful-by-any-other-metric businesses.

Why does this happen? The venture capital business is a high-risk, high-return investment strategy in which venture funds swap capital for early-stage startup equity, essentially buying a piece of the future value of the companies in which they invest. For the model to work, the rare winners like Uber, Airbnb, and Stripe need to pay for all the losers. Aileen Lee of Cowboy Ventures coined the term "unicorn" to refer to privately held startups valued at more than $1 billion, which are the lifeblood of venture funds. In fairy tales, people can't help chasing unicorns—they are nearly irresistible, but they're also rare, elusive, and nearly impossible to catch.

Her mythological metaphor couldn't have been more apt. Almost everyone fails to build billion-dollar businesses, even the founders who raise gobs of venture capital. According to Matt Murphy, managing director and partner of Menlo Ventures, approximately 70 percent of startups fail, which can mean anything from full liquidation to becoming cash flow positive, which, despite being good for the company, is still bad for the VC. Of the 30 percent still standing, he says, some return three to five times the initial investment, which constitutes only modest success in this setting. The whole system is riding on at least 5 percent of VC-backed companies delivering tenfold to one hundredfold returns to balance out losses and make it all worth it. Without them, the VC model simply doesn't work. That's because the outsized success of the rare billion-dollar startup compensates for all the money thrown against the wall, like so much spaghetti, on thousands of other ventures.

That's not what minimalist entrepreneurs do. We are laser focused on profitability from day one, in order to get to sustainability soon after, so that we can serve our customers and our communities for as long as we wish.

Don't Call It a Comeback

No matter where you work, how you work, or who you work for right now, you can use the principles in this book to re-think the beliefs and practices that may be holding you back. I really do believe that starting a business should be an option for everyone, no matter your background. That's why this book is full of examples of many great businesses that have been built by passionate individuals around the world, many who have flown under the radar until now. For up-and-coming minimalist entrepreneurs, I hope their stories can serve as examples as new online tools make the process of building, marketing, and selling easier and cheaper for everyone—including solopreneurs and independent creators.

Where do you start? Take a good hard look at the people, places, and communities you care about. Where are the pain points? What isn't working, but might with a little elbow grease? These are all opportunities to make things better through minimalist entrepreneurship. It's ironic to me how often people go around hoping to find a startup idea while si-multaneously complaining about all the everyday stuff around them that doesn't work properly. "Sure, I could solve that for people with a little effort, but the potential market just isn't big enough to really scale." That's the kind of thinking that this book seeks to address.

You may already be on your business-building journey, but if you're just getting started, some business models lend themselves more easily to the pathway of minimalist entre-preneurship. These include almost any kind of business-to-consumer or business-to-business enterprise that has fast customer feedback loops and ample opportunities for iteration like software as a service (SaaS), digital and physical products and services, or connecting people for a fee. We'll talk about all of these later in the book.

There are also businesses that aren't necessarily suited for this framework because of the slow pace of customer feedback. For example, any business that requires a heavy investment in research and development or that relies on sales to large, bureaucratized corporations or institutions—like Fortune 100 companies, academia, or hospitals—might not match up as well with the processes and systems I recommend.

The good news is that what constitutes a "business" is changing faster than ever before and opening up possibilities to a wider range of innovators. Though this shift was in motion before 2020, the COVID-19 pandemic accelerated it and drove increased interest in entrepreneurship from people of all backgrounds. Now more than ever before, we don't need to move to a place called Silicon Valley, go to a school called Harvard or Stanford, and raise money from the venture capitalists. The internet lets you learn from anywhere, network with anyone, and raise money directly from customers.

The world desperately needs the solutions that only entrepreneurs can provide. Everyday problems are all around us, but they are often hidden from the view of the Silicon Valley software engineers and Ivy League overachievers who have been anointed as our entrepreneurial class. We need the help of entrepreneurs from every part of the planet and every stratum of society. It's down to individual creators and entrepreneurs to set better goals for ourselves and our businesses. After all, problems don't solve themselves. People do.

Creator First, Entrepreneur Second

On paper, it seems simple enough:

1. Narrow down who your ideal customer is. Narrow until you can narrow no more.
2. Define exactly what pain point you are solving for them, and how much they will pay you to solve it.
3. Set a hard deadline and focus fully on building a solution, then charge for it.
4. Repeat the process until you've found a product that works, then scale a business around it.

In practice, it's not so simple. There are many complications that pop up, and most people don't even know where to start. A "business" of any kind is too scary, too amorphous, or too unattainable. Luckily, there's another way to get started today. Before you become an entrepreneur, become a creator.

That could mean being an artist, but it doesn't have to. Creators make things, charge their audiences for those things, and then use that money to make more things. They use the first dollars they earn as tools to fuel their own creative drive, not the other way around. With time and experience, creators show others how to turn their own creativity into businesses, and the cycle continues. In the end, there isn't much difference between a business like Gumroad and a creator. It's just semantics—one or more people using the tool of a business to make something new. Painters need brushes. Writers need pencils. Creators need businesses. It's key for people to understand that, because it lowers the cognitive barrier to starting a business, and starting is *really* important. You don't learn, then start. You start, then learn.

My best friend in middle school, obsessed with the computer game *World of Warcraft*, started designing fantasy creatures in Photoshop. I was impressed, but I also remember thinking, "I could do that." So I went through some Photoshop tutorials and got to work. When I started to get the hang of the software, I began submitting logos to online competitions. I didn't win any, but the process of creating a lot of stuff and putting it out there made me a pretty decent designer, and then led to freelance web design work.

Once you're working on other people's projects, you can't help but get ideas of your own, so I began building simple web applications, hiring developers to help with the coding. For example, before Twitter natively supported threads, I created an app called Tweader to see the conversations that happened between people on Twitter. Another app, Ping Me When It's Up, would text me when a website that had gone down was back up again. (It should be clear by now that I've never been very good at naming things.)

When the iPhone App Store opened, I learned to code for it by taking a free course on iOS development from Stanford through iTunes University, called CS193P (I still recommend it!). The App Store handled all the financial aspects of selling what I made to customers around the world, which meant I could focus on creating apps. Perfect.

The first app I built was called Taxi Lah!, which let users call a cab from their phones—before Uber. I put it on the App Store for fellow Singaporeans and made a few thousand dollars. Then I made an app called Color Stream that let designers create and modify color palettes on their phones. I made about $10,000 from that. Each time, I was trying to solve a problem I had. I wanted to design and build a little bit of software to make my life—and the lives of others—a little bit better.

This experience—shipping real products to real customers—led to my first job at Pinterest, where I designed and built the Pinterest iPhone app. While I was there, I built Gumroad in my spare time to help me sell an icon I designed in Photoshop. When I found a solution that worked, I sold it to other creators, who sold their products to their own community of creators, many of whom eventually became Gumroad customers themselves. Now I'm an honest-to-goodness entrepreneur without ever having really given it much conscious thought along the way.

The App Store cleared the marketing and financial obstacles out of my way so that I could fully embrace my creative side and become a creator. That transition led to me becoming a founder. It's an upward, virtuous cycle. Creation begets more creation. Today, Gumroad does the exact same thing for other would-be creators. It's basically a glorified Sahil-cloning factory. Isn't that beautiful? (My mom thinks it is.)

Max Ulichney is an art director and illustrator based in Los Angeles. He'd always imagined he'd spend his days working at a large company to pay the bills in return for a few hours in the evening to do his own work. He spent fifteen years as an art director at the same creative agency, eventually using an iPad app called Procreate to draw and paint in between meetings. One day, a couple of years ago, Max decided to sell some of the digital "brushes" he'd designed for his own use to other Procreate users. A few hundred dollars later, he decided it was worth the effort to continue selling the digital tools as a business. Two years in, Max was making a living as an independent creator. Recently, he quit his job at the agency to work on Maxpacks full-time.

There are thousands of "creator first, entrepreneur second" stories like Max's.

Adam Wathan and Steve Schoger teach people how to build and design web applications. They believe, as I do, that nearly anyone can become a competent front-end engineer and designer with a little help. In December 2018, after just a few years building their online audiences, they released Refactoring UI, an online course, earning over $800,000 in a single month. Now they get to spend their time doing what they really love: building Tailwind, a free and open-source framework for the rapid creation of custom web designs.

Kristina Garner, mother of two boys, teaches families how to run secular, nature-based homeschooling programs for their kids. What started as a blog in 2015 about her personal passion has become Blossom and Root, a business that employs dozens of people and helps thousands of families every month.

These are just a few of the 28,207 creators who sold something on Gumroad last month. That sounds like a big number today, but I too started somewhere smaller and less lofty, where creation always begins: at the number next to zero. Where there was nothing, now there's something: digital brushes, online courses, Vidalia onions on your doorstep.

In the next chapter, I'll show you how to get started.

KEY TAKEAWAYS

o You don't learn, then start. You start, then learn.
o Minimalist entrepreneurs focus on getting "profitable at all costs" instead of growing at all costs.
o A business is a way to solve problems for people you care about—and get paid for it.
o Become a creator first, an entrepreneur second.

Learn More

○ Follow Peter Askew (@searchbound) on Twitter, where he regularly tweets about business ideas, domain name opportunities, and other interesting stuff.

○ Read his article "I Sell Onions on the Internet" at www.deepsouthventures.com/i-sell-onions-on-the-internet/.

○ Read the article that inspired this book: "Reflecting on My Failure to Build a Billion-Dollar Company" at sahillavingia.com/reflecting.

○ Follow @gumroad on Instagram to see our creators' stories.

○ Join the Minimalist Entrepreneurs club on Clubhouse to meet and learn from other minimalist entrepreneurs in the community.

2

start with community

It takes a village to raise a child.

—AFRICAN PROVERB

In 2009, Sol Orwell was overweight and unhappy, so he decided to join the "r/Fitness" subreddit, one of the thousands of smaller online communities within Reddit, to find information and support. At the same time, he started reading about fitness and nutrition, taking notes on what he was learning in books like Tim Ferriss's *The 4-Hour Body* and posting summaries on the fitness subreddit for other members of the community. Reddit was a natural place for Orwell to seek connection. He was already participating in the NBA and Toronto subreddits, among others, so he knew and understood Reddit's rules and norms about posting only authentic, useful content.

The more he learned about fitness and nutrition, the more he shared. In addition to his reading notes, he inspired others by answering questions and documenting his personal journey of losing sixty pounds, which occurred over a period of several years. He credits his physical transformation to the relationships he formed with other "redditors," including Kurtis Frank, one of the moderators of r/Fitness. Eventually, Sol and Kurtis ended up moderating the subreddit together, and as time went by, they noticed two persistent problems.

First, little reliable information was available about nutritional supplements, either from other redditors or from the companies that made these products; second, almost every day, new members asked the same questions over and over again, many times about supplements. Sol was frustrated by both situations, but eventually he realized that maybe the resources people needed just weren't out there.

Sol and Kurtis saw a job to be done for a community that they cared about and had nurtured from five thousand to about fifty thousand during the two years they had been moderating. In 2011, they launched Examine.com, a website where people could find the kind of free, unbiased, up-to-date research and information on nutrition and supplements that they themselves had been looking for.

They told people about their project, but they didn't sell anything, and they only occasionally dropped links in the fitness subreddit when they were answering questions. Instead, other members of the community did it for them. After all, they had been part of Reddit at this point for about five years. Sol remembers they both had something like "100,000 plus karma," a measure of how much a user has contributed to Reddit based on upvotes and comments from other users— so people trusted them, and they were solving a problem for the fitness subreddit without asking for anything in return.

In 2013, two years after they started the site, they started to think about monetizing, so they surveyed the community about what problems they believed the information on

Examine.com might be able to solve. "We would ask people, 'What's your problem? What do you wish you could do?'" Sol remembers. "The most common thing was 'We wish you just had a table of all of the information you have. So if I wanted to look at supplements that affect blood pressure, I could look it up quickly.'" Because of those answers, they offered their first product, the *Research Digest*, a comprehensive guide to supplements and nutrition.

Sol was well known in the health and nutrition space, and to promote the Research Digest, he leveraged his relationships with fitness professionals *four years* after initially joining the fitness subreddit. When he and Kurtis launched, 105 people in the fitness industry shared the link. The goal was a thousand sales, and by the end of the first day they had already sold six to eight hundred copies. By the end of the launch, they had sold three thousand copies, all based on reputation, trust, and word of mouth.

Fast-forward to today, and Sol is happy, healthy, and wealthy. Examine.com continues to be an important resource for health and nutrition professionals; it has seventy thousand visitors per day and does seven figures in annual revenue, though Sol has since stepped back from the day-to-day operations. The team has expanded Examine's offerings to include additional guides and subscription services on how supplements factor not only into fitness but also into longevity, chronic disease, and psychological health. But they've never lost their focus on community and continue to depend on the trust and relationships that grew authentically over time.

In this chapter, we'll talk about how you can find your own communities (if you haven't already) and how to uncover the kinds of problems that might be best suited for a minimalist business. I won't lie. This process takes time, but done right and, most of all, done authentically, it will be the basis of how you move forward now and for years to come. Whether you're just getting started or you're already in the process of building a product, knowing and contributing to your community is key at every stage. Remember that, and you'll find and nurture the right atmosphere for collaboration, growth, and eventually a sustainable business that matters.

Community First

Community is a fundamental societal unit. From Sol's r/Fitness subreddit to yoga classes to family to the group of friends we game with in the middle of the night, communities are a place where we can connect, learn, and have fun. For minimalist entrepreneurs, communities are the starting point of any successful enterprise.

That doesn't mean you should run out and find a community to join just for the purpose of starting a business. It means that most businesses fail because they aren't built with a particular group of people in mind. Often, the ones that succeed do so because they're focused on a community that a founder knows well. That process can't be rushed because it comes from authentic relationships and a willingness to serve, both of which take time to uncover and develop. You may even have to learn a new language—or at least some insider lingo.

Communities used to be limited by geography, but it's never been easier to connect to people with whom you share something in common, whether it be an interest, a favorite artist, or a belief system. But a community isn't a group of people who all think, act, look, or behave the same. That's a cult.

A community is the opposite. That's what I discovered when I moved from San Francisco to Provo and got out of the Silicon Valley bubble. For one of the first times in my life, I saw that the best communities are made up of individuals who might be otherwise dissimilar but who have shared interests, values, and abilities. It's a group of people who would likely never hang out with each other in any other situational context, and it often encompasses virtually every identity, including, yes, politics.

A community can override people's dislike of one another. Every Sunday in the Latter-day Saints Church, I saw the progressive next to the conservative, the rich next to the poor, the young next to the old. I'm not sure what they thought of each other outside the church building, but for at least one day a week, they sat together for the sake of the community.

It wasn't easy. It was real work to be an active participant in that church community, to learn how to speak the language, but for the first time in a long time, I was reminded of something important: you don't have to bring your whole self to every community you join, but you do have to bring a slice of yourself. And that part needs to be authentic to its core. It's the combination of time and vulnerability that leads to relationships and growth.

Part of my own growth was realizing that as an outsider, I was in a particularly great position to see the community with fresh eyes and to contribute value in a new way. You may never move to a new city, but getting out of your bubble matters when it comes to community. And it's healthy and normal to leave certain communities as you explore new ones.

You don't have to bring your whole self to every community you join, but you do have to bring a slice of yourself.

For me, my move from Silicon Valley to the Silicon Slopes showed me that I didn't care too much about tech, at least not in the way that I thought I did. In Utah, I didn't go to Java-Script meetups or attend design lectures or judge startup pitch competitions. Instead, I found myself at figure drawing classes. Or a few hundred feet away from a barn, learning how to plein-air paint. Or at a coffee shop on Thursday mornings, writing and reviewing science-fiction stories with a few friends I met at a workshop.

Finding these creative communities in real life reminded me of the spark that inspired me in the early days. And rediscovering myself as a creator and spending time with other makers reconnected me to why I had built Gumroad in the first place: I loved to create! I couldn't believe I had forgotten that, for years.

I was accidentally at the forefront of a movement that was taking shape—what Li Jin, former partner at Andreessen Horowitz and founder of Atelier Ventures, calls the "passion economy"—"a world in which people are able to do what they love for a living and to have a more fulfilling and purposeful life." At the time I created Gumroad, online creator platforms were still new, but the rise of no-code solutions has made building and charging for podcasts, video and audio content, online courses, virtual teaching, and virtual coaching almost seamless, so that starting a business around something you love has never been more attainable.

You probably have something you enjoy, something that on its face has nothing to do with your "real" job. Maybe it's marathon running or ceramics or electronic music or another passion that you pursue in your free time. Whatever it is, building a minimalist business around the people you love to spend time with and the ways you love to spend your time depends on being part of a community. You may already be thinking about how to solve the problems of a current community you participate in, or you may simply be planning to join a community based on something you love. Either way, finding your people is really important at the beginning. Not just for the sake of your business but also for the sake of your own well-being.

Taking writing and painting classes in Provo reminded me that my community wasn't just the people in front of me; it was also a wider group who wanted, like me, to "turn their passions into livelihoods." The real communities I was a part of didn't care about growth at all costs; that kind of accelerated expansion would have cracked them into a million little pieces. Instead, their priority, like mine, was connecting to each other in ways that allowed for the space, time, and freedom to explore their interests and to eventually transform their passions into businesses in meaningful ways.

Find Your People

Many people struggle to consciously place themselves within communities, even though everyone is *already* a part of several. If you're reading this and wondering which communities you're already a part of, ask yourself these questions:

If I talk, who listens?

Where and with whom do I already spend my time, online and offline?

In what situations am I most authentically myself?

Who do I hang out with, even though I don't really like them, but it's worth it since we share something more important in common?

Spend an hour, at least. Let yourself think you've run out of ideas at least a few times. In the list you end up creating, you'll find the people you are meant to serve. You may be tempted to skip this exercise if you've already started a business, but I believe that doing this regularly is a good opportunity to remind yourself why you're doing what you're doing and, most important, who you're doing it for.

From here, you can turn your list of communities into a list of locations—geographic and online—in which to spend even more time learning and contributing:

o For every group with a shared interest, there's a Facebook group, a Reddit community, a Twitter or Instagram hashtag, or some other form of gathering and sharing ideas on the web. There are often several. Join them all.

o There are communities run by the businesses that service that community: forums, groups, and more. Join those too.

o There are also notable teachers, with online classes that also function as communities. They may be also worth joining—though be mindful of the cost.

o Of course, there are the in-person communities! There are meetups, workshops, classes, speaker series, networking events, and more.

It's important to note that your goal here is to join *communities*, not networks.

In a network, such as Facebook, Twitter, or Instagram, newcomers start at zero. No one says "hi" when they walk in the door, and if you have something to say, there's no guarantee that anyone will hear or help.

Networks, in person or online, aren't bad. Sometimes they can lead to genuine and meaningful connection, especially

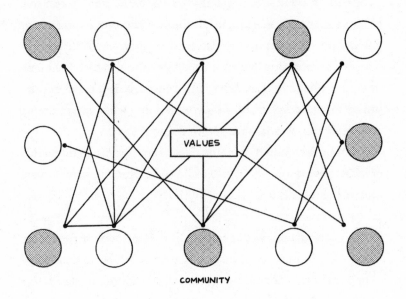

COMMUNITY

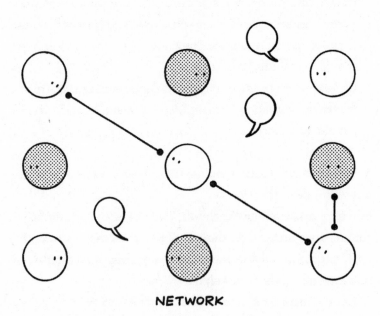

NETWORK

over time, as you gain friends and followers and the algorithms start to recommend your work and your content to people who don't already know you. But where did those friends and followers come from in the first place? The communities you're in! (Note: Networks and audience are really important for the minimalist entrepreneur, just not yet. We'll cover them deeply in chapter 5.)

Eventually, you will be part of various networks as the face of your business, but at the beginning, beware of believing that communities and networks are interchangeable, no matter how appealing the potential virality may seem. Instead, build deep relationships first.

Contribute, Create, and Teach

Being a member of a community is a start, but the real magic happens when you start to contribute. Authors and bloggers Ben McConnell and Jackie Huba call this the "1% Rule": On the internet, they say, 1 percent create, 9 percent contribute, and 90 percent consume. They've shown this rule to be true when applied to sites like Wikipedia and Yahoo, and it's also widely applicable to other collaborative websites. For example, most people do not post, comment, or even upvote on Reddit like Sol Orwell and Kurtis Frank did. Instead they browse anonymously, which is known as "lurking." To cite one example, even when the r/Askreddit subreddit was getting 1.5 million unique visitors a day, it was only getting 2,674 submissions and 110,408 comments in the same period.

If you contribute, you will have ten times the presence of someone who doesn't. And it will continue to grow from there.

Contributing means commenting, editing, and generally being part of the broader conversation. What's more, if you

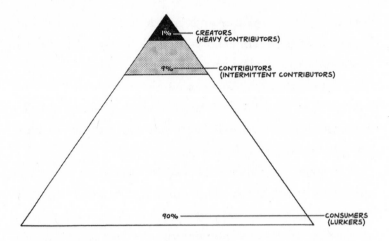

go further and create by showing what you're working on, teaching what you're learning, and bringing new material to your community, that influence will grow ninetyfold. Of course I am simplifying, but hopefully the point stands: While it's better to lurk rather than needlessly comment, it's even better to add value into the community *even if you don't feel that you're ready.* If you struggle with this, as many do, remind yourself that if you have something to add, it's selfish to keep it to yourself!

Once you begin contributing, folks will start recognizing your name. Eventually, some may seek your words of wisdom by "@mention"ing you directly or by following you so they get notified every time you post.

When I lived in Utah, I met several painters who built communities and eventually businesses in this way. One example is landscape oil painter Bryan Mark Taylor, who was part of a community of painters and art enthusiasts participating in and attending plein-air painting competitions up and down the California coastline. He sold his work through these competitions and established a loyal group of collectors and fellow artists, who followed him to Instagram. There he grew his community by posting more of his work and educational videos. When his easel broke on a backpacking trip in the early 2010s, he created the first prototype of the Strada Easel to solve his own problem. And because his community had grown organically over a period of years and through a shared passion, he had thousands of other painters he could share it with who then wanted one for themselves. Today, the Strada Easel makes him and his employees a happy living, and he gets to paint as much as he wants.

Once you're regularly cultivating relationships by contributing to the conversation, the time will come when you're ready to go further and educate others. But what will you say and how will you engage the people you've come to know and respect in your community? It's all about creating value and can all be summed up by three signs Nathan Barry, the founder of ConvertKit, which provides email marketing for creators, has hanging in his office. They read:

o "Work in Public"
o "Teach Everything You Know"
o "Create Every Day"

If you're always learning, you'll always have something to teach others about their own next best steps.

When Nathan started blogging and publishing ebooks in 2006, he struggled to grow the community for his work, while others in his space seemed to have no trouble at all. One web designer he followed was Chris Coyier, who was regularly posting articles and tutorials on his website, CSS-Tricks.com.

Chris had a following based on his articles, and in 2012 when he needed $3,500 for living expenses to take a month off to redesign his site, he promised recorded tutorials about the redesign process in exchange for a contribution to his Kickstarter campaign. In short order, Chris raised $87,000. "I couldn't help but think how Chris and I had equal skill sets when it came to web design," Nathan writes. "We started at the same time and progressed at the same rate. So how did Chris have the ability to flip the switch and make $87,000 off a Kickstarter campaign and I didn't have the ability at all? What was the difference?"

They were both doing the work, but Chris was sharing it, while Nathan was not. "I realized I would take on a project, do the work, deliver the project and move on," he said. "Chris did the same thing, BUT before he moved on, he would teach about everything he learned doing that project. When he could, he shared samples, he wrote tutorials about the code he wrote and any specific methods he went through. He did this with every project. The difference was that all along the way, Chris was teaching everything he knew and I wasn't." Since that epiphany, ConvertKit has grown to over $20 million in annual recurring revenue.

Chances are, if you've learned something, there's probably a good portion of your community that would find value in learning that same thing from you, even if you aren't the world's leading authority on the subject.

And if you're regularly learning, then you'll always have regular content to contribute to the community. This can become a nice flywheel over time, as teaching often becomes the best way to drive your own curiosity and inspiration to learn more yourself. And when you learn publicly, your students will have questions that force you to learn even more stuff to teach them.

You don't have to teach *everything* you learn. In fact, a

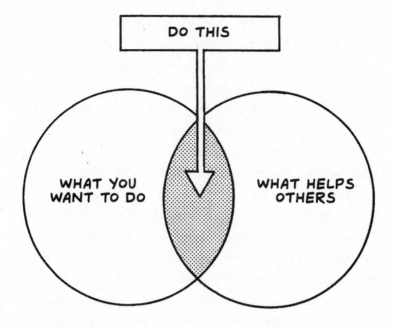

narrower core focus can be better. For example, Patrick Mc-Kenzie, a writer, entrepreneur, and software business expert who is best known for a 2012 post on salary negotiation that has since become a cult classic in the software engineering space, believes that the best personal brands exist at the intersection of two topics. He now works for Stripe, where he continues to write and advise software engineers and software entrepreneurs about how to start and scale their businesses, speaking from real experience as a creator and business owner himself.

If you're learning every day, which you probably are, you'll have something to share every day. Meanwhile, you'll build your skills and experience, learn to speak the language, and grow your community, all essential ingredients when you eventually have a product you are ready to sell.

Unfortunately, as you probably already know, there are no

shortcuts. As you think about what you're creating now and how that might lead to a business in the future, look to the communities you're already a part of. You've invested time and energy there, so perhaps you already have an idea of how to proceed. If you don't, keep going, and continue using your time to get strong, to learn how to paint, to learn how to code, to learn how to write, or to learn whatever else you are into, teaching what you're learning along the way.

When you are proficient enough to monetize what you know, now or in the future, if you've put in the time, you will be part of a sizable community that will eventually be your first group of prospective customers (more on that in chapters 4 and 5). This is an important factor in keeping you honest about the quality of work you are able to produce. Your community should serve as proof that you're improving, producing, and helping others; these people could spend their attention on a gazillion things, and they've chosen you.

Becoming a person who helps people precedes building a business that helps people. It's not a coincidence. When you become a pillar in a community, you gain exposure to the problems that the people within it face. People will come to you, explain their problems, and ask for your help in solving them.

Overnight Success Is a Myth

It took me a long time—until writing this book!—to realize how important communities were to my career. The Gumroad origin story I tell starts with me working as an early engineer at Pinterest. A few months in, on a Friday night, I was at home learning how to design a photorealistic icon for a side project. I came up with this:

I spent four hours, if I recall correctly. But if I had had a source file to work from, something to see how all the shadows and highlights and shapes came together, it would have taken me half that time. I would have totally paid money for that, at least a buck. And because I was part of a community of like-minded designers, I knew many others would too. Not only that, but a subset of those designers followed me directly on Twitter—all potential customers.

I looked around online, assuming it was going to be incredibly easy to sell something digital to my audience, but it wasn't. It would have required setting up a whole storefront and paying a monthly fee. I had stubbed my toe on a problem—a concept we'll explore in more detail later in this chapter.

I built Gumroad that weekend, launched it Monday morning, and even sold a few copies of that pencil icon.

But the classic origin story is incomplete. It turns out I had had a similar problem and thought process before, but I hadn't decided to build Gumroad then. In a blog post from 2012, I wrote about trying unsuccessfully to find a way to sell the source code for a Twitter client app I built for the iPhone. I searched for a solution for a few hours, but I couldn't find anything and gave up.

A lot had changed in the years between the first time I imagined what would eventually become Gumroad and the second time, but the most important shift was that I had found my communities and had established myself within them by creating, contributing, learning, and teaching. When I had the idea the second time around, I was armed with the confidence, audience, and insights to solve a meaningful problem quickly and effectively.

From the outside, it all seems so straightforward, but it took time not only to become part of the community but also to choose the community I wanted to serve and decide on the problem I wanted to solve. There's really no such thing as overnight success. Most are years in the making, just like my ability to build Gumroad over a weekend was also many years in the works.

When I was just getting started with web design, parents and teachers were my first clients (a social studies teacher needed a website for her books, while a parent needed help with the online presence of a local charity auction). Over time, I found like-minded web designers on web forums like TalkFreelance, self-described as a "forum for web designers and freelance developers" interested in website design, programming, search engine optimization, and more. Later, I found Hacker News, a site where most of Silicon Valley congregated online. At first, I was a lurker, then a commenter, and then an active contributor. And because my Twitter account was in my profile, as well as in my email signature, I started to collect a small following of people who signaled their interest in following *me*!

Communities were essential for my personal development and career growth. They were where I made friends and formed business relationships. To this day, I am still meeting people who remember my name or handle from those years. I never had an agenda. I just knew I wanted to be part of Hacker News. And with their help, when I launched Gumroad that first Monday morning, it rocketed to the top of the front page of the site and stayed there all day. Even though that was just the beginning of my story, it was still confirmation that I had found my people and was where I belonged.

Picking the Right Community

Once you are part of a community, you can start to make a list of difficulties its members face, and you can think about how you could build a product or service to solve one or more of them.

Every community has a unique set of problems that's calling out for a custom-built solution. You're probably part of a number of communities, but when it comes to making an impact in a community in a way that leads to a minimalist business, you should focus on a community where you can (and want to): (1) create long-term value; (2) build relationships for decades to come; and (3) carve out a unique, authentic voice for yourself. For the minimalist entrepreneur trying to make an impact, community is a way to stay focused: Instead of changing the world, you can change your community's world.

It's not enough to pick any community; you also have to consider your own interests. There are many communities that you may be a part of, but that doesn't mean you want to dedicate a significant portion of your waking hours to solving their problems. Unless some element of the community and its problems overlap with something you're passionate about, it is unlikely you would be happy operating a business within the space—contempt for your customers is not optimal.

There are two more important attributes that will decide which is the ideal community to focus on: how large the community is, and how much money they are willing to spend (said differently: the total addressable market, or TAM). The goal here is not to find the largest community with the most dollars to spend in order to capture 1 percent of it. Instead, you should find something right in the middle. Too small, and you won't be able to build a sustainable business. Too large, and it will cost too much money to get to sustainability in the first place—and you will attract or create competitors along the way, leading to a race to the bottom in product pricing that you may not survive.

The best way to win is to be the only. And the best way to be the only is to pick a group that is Goldilocks size, has problems they would pay money to solve, and is underserved (likely because it is too small for larger competitors to go after).

Tope Awotona, founder of Calendly, started three very different companies for three completely different communities before eventually building the scheduling software business in 2013. In 2020, Calendly posted nearly $70 million in annual recurring revenue, more than double its 2019 figure. But Awotona's first company was a dating app that never really got off the ground. The second was projectorspot.com, which sold (obviously) projectors, but sales were poor and margins small. He tried again with a third startup, selling grills, but as he says, "I didn't know anything about grills and I didn't want to! I lived in an apartment, and never even grilled." Not only was he not part of the grilling community, but he didn't even want to be!

He took a different approach to building Calendly. He had been a sales rep earlier in his career, and he knew the hassle of sending multiple emails to schedule meetings. He had even run into the scheduling problem while trying to sell his own products as an entrepreneur. As time went on and his other ideas failed to gain traction, he saw a gap in the marketplace and resolved to address it for the community of sales reps he cared about and understood. He says that "the journey to creating something that's impactful, something that serves people, something that you know people are willing to open up their wallets and pay for—is not something that you can do just for money." While lots of people have scheduling fatigue, Awotona focused on problems specific to sales reps, which helped him define a problem he could both solve *and* monetize.

What does that mean for you? First, get involved in those communities wherever they are, offline and online. Then, contribute, teach, and, most important, listen. Finally, use the filters above to make sure you are picking the right community to serve.

Then, your problem becomes: *Which problem should I pick?*

Picking the Right Problem to Solve

The late Clayton Christensen described picking the right problem to solve as an opportunity to help customers achieve what they hope to achieve in a particular moment. "What [great companies] really need to home in on," he wrote in a 2016 article for *Harvard Business Review,* "is the progress that the customer is trying to make in a given circumstance— what the customer hopes to accomplish: the job to be done."

For example, millions of people buy McDonald's milkshakes. Why? Because McDonald's found out that the job to be done was to accompany lonely drivers on their trips to work. "Nearly half the milkshakes were sold in the very early morning. It was the only thing [the customers] bought, they were always alone, and they always got in the car and drove off with it." This is one reason why McDonald's milkshakes are so viscous: so they last a whole, lonely car ride.

Now, the McDonald's marketing team can go into an office

and create a problem that could potentially be solved only by their food. Then they can spend hundreds of millions of dollars on advertising to convince people that they have this problem, and that they too could "hire" a milkshake to get the job done.

Christensen's idea of "the job to be done" is sound, but McDonald's is doing it in the wrong order. They didn't start with the customer; they started with the job to be done, and then sank a ton of money into making customers believe they needed that job to be done.

Minimalist entrepreneurs don't have millions of dollars, nor do they want to manufacture problems for people. Instead, we believe that people already have enough problems, and that our role is to help them get rid of one.

That is why it is so key to start with community. If you try to make something for everyone, you will likely end up making something that no one really wants or needs. Once you know the group of people you want to help, you will start to see their problems much more readily. There are more problems than businesses. You just have to find them.

Still struggling? Grab a pen and paper. On the left, write down the person/community you would like to help. In the center, write down how they spend their time (buying onions, making icons of pencils on a Friday night, painting). On the right, write down the problems with each activity. It might look like the figure on page 46.

That blankness is like a blank canvas, or a blank page, or a blank business plan. You want to start a business to solve a problem, but you don't have any problems to solve.

If you're struggling here (many do), some Economics 101 may help. There are only four different types of utility: *place utility, form utility, time utility,* and *possession utility.* What

PERSON	HOBBY/ACTIVITY	PROBLEM
WIFE		
MOM		
PAINTERS	PAINTING	
ME		

can you make easier to understand, faster to get, cheaper to buy, or more accessible to others?

○ Place utility: Make something inaccessible accessible
○ Form utility: Make something more valuable by rearranging existing parts
○ Time utility: Make something slow go fast
○ Possession utility: Remove a middleman

PLACE UTILITY: MAKE SOMETHING INACCESSIBLE ACCESSIBLE

FORM UTILITY: MAKE SOMETHING MORE VALUABLE BY REARRANGING EXISTING PARTS

TIME UTILITY: MAKE SOMETHING SLOW GO FAST

POSSESSION UTILITY: REMOVE A MIDDLEMAN

You are not trying to *create* problems for people in order to solve them, à la McDonald's. You are trying to discover inefficiencies in the lives of people you care about so you can help them. These may sound abstract, so let's put the four types of utility in context.

A business that farms coffee beans in Ecuador and sells them in San Francisco is changing the "place" property of the beans. Place utility is what you are paying the premium for.

If a coffee shop buys beans from a wholesaler and grinds them up, their customers are paying a premium for form utility. (They are also, in theory, paying a premium for place utility if the coffee shop is closer to them than the distributor is. Of course, many businesses are a combination.)

If they also sell croissants that would take you three days to make, you are also paying a premium for time utility.

Finally, if you decide it's better for you to invest in a croissant-making machine to make your own croissants than to pay for them over and over again, that's possession utility.

One business that provides time utility is theCut, an app that connects barbers and clients and makes it faster and easier to find, book, and pay for services. Founders Obi Omile and Kush Patel came up with the idea after spending hours struggling to find barbers they liked and trusted. And getting an appointment with the best barbers often meant waiting hours because many used informal booking systems. TheCut provides utility for both sides. Clients save time, and barbers find new clients (possession utility), spend less time communicating with current ones (time utility), and receive mobile payments (form utility).

Omile and Patel built a great business because they understood the problems that plagued the community they planned to serve. Once you've picked your own community, the path to the right solution will become clear for you too.

Solving Your Own Problem

Everyone has problems, "stubbing their toe" throughout their day. You may look around and think your life is pretty good, and maybe the folks around you do too. Or maybe the problems are obvious, and you already know what you want to build.

But most people, from my experience, miss these moments when they get whiplash from something being much harder or more painful than they initially expected. The brain adapts

quickly, assuming the new state of things. It's *meant* to be this hard, it thinks, or there's a really good reason that it is, or it would be too annoying to change. I think that's the wrong way to go about life. Life is getting better all the time, and you can help accelerate the pace.

Basecamp had their own version of this moment when they were struggling to find the right tool to manage products with their clients. As founder Jason Fried says, "We went looking for a tool to do this. What we found were ancient relics. To us, project management was all about communication. None of the software makers at the time seemed to agree. So we decided to make our own."

When they launched, they were already an essential part of the online product management and web design community, with a well-read blog and dozens of clients. How did this help them?

In Jason's words: "We decided early on that if we were able to generate around $5,000/month after a year (or about $60,000 in annual revenue), we'd have a good thing going. Turns out, we hit that number in about six weeks. So we absolutely were on to something." When they had something ready to show their community, it turned out that many members had encountered the same roadblock.

If you have a problem, other people probably do too. Like many chefs, Nick Kokonas regularly faced the issue of lost revenue from no-shows at his Chicago restaurants. In a bid to solve his own problem, he cofounded Tock, which manages demand through traditional reservations but also through ticketing, which allows diners to prepay for reservations and special events and permits restaurants to create "demand pricing" based on the desirability of reservation times. Prior to 2020, Tock was in thirty countries and two hundred cities, and was in use by thousands of restaurants, including some of the world's best. During the COVID-19 pandemic, Tock innovated further by launching Tock to Go, which allows customers to reserve and purchase restaurant meals for pickup from restaurants that may not have offered takeout or delivery ever before.

All of these businesses and many, many more hark back to community as a starting point. After all, if the problem you are solving for other people is also one you are solving for yourself, you will be able to kill a lot of birds with one stone. And if you build a product to solve your own problem, you will have at least one user—more than most startups ever get. Plus, you can talk to that user every single second of the day!

Building the Right Solution

Most businesses do not work, even if they are solving a real problem. This is often because while they are building something people want, they are not building it in the right way with the right minimalist mindset. So what kind of business can you build without a dollar of venture capital, appropriate to your skills and resources, in line with your mission, and viable in the marketplace?

It is also important to ask: If your business achieves its potential, what kind of positive impact might it make on the world? That, not the lure of an IPO, should be the guiding light for the founders of a company and all of its employees.

These are the criteria I use:

o **Will I love it?** Building a business is hard and time-consuming. It will take years. And the more successful it is, the longer you will work on it. So it's important to find something you *want* to work on, for people you *want* to work for. To build a successful business, you need to build something people love. To stick with it, you need to build something *you* love working on.

o **Will it be inherently monetizable?** There should be a clear path to charging people money for something of value, in a way that feels obvious. If it makes sense, it'll make cents.

o **Does it have an internal growth mechanism?** In 2020, Gumroad's revenues almost doubled due solely to word of mouth. In our case, it's impossible to use the product without sharing it with other people, and as a result, we've been able to "outsource" our sales and marketing efforts because our customer base does the work for us as their customers use our platform. This is true of a lot of minimalist businesses, especially because you're going to build a great product people want to tell others about, and that they may eventually want to use themselves.

o **Do I have the right natural skill sets to build this business?** For example, if the business requires a lot of business development or sales calls to get off the ground, and you are deathly scared of speaking to anyone, then it's probably not a good fit for you. There are a lot of businesses waiting to be built—pick the right one for you.

No one book contains everything you'll need to know for starting any kind of business. The important thing is the thought process you bring to figuring things out for yourself. You need the right mindset and to know what questions to ask yourself. It begins and ends by thinking of your business as a tool to solve a customer's problem. Not as a lottery ticket.

Squashing Your Doubts

Finally, even though you have an idea you are excited about and are confident you can build, at some point you will have doubts. Surround yourself with colleagues and mentors who will not only tell you the truth but will also encourage you when the going gets tough. After all, people need cheerleaders, not just advice. Inspiring (and inspired) founders and leaders are not born, they are made. Almost anyone can do it, with enough patience, guidance, and sincerity.

A minimalist business can meet you where you are. It can grow with you as you grow (more on this in chapter 6). I would be lying if I said talent didn't matter at all, but what truly makes great founders and great businesses in the long term is a great deal of persistence. And one way to maximize your chances of success is to focus on a smaller product, on a community you are a core part of, and to be honest about whether you are solving the problem effectively or not. That's why a mindful approach to selling to a community you already have a relationship with is so important.

When you have doubts—and you will have doubts—go back to the fact that you've already started the work. By now, you will have (1) zeroed in on a mission-aligned problem to solve and (2) generated feasible ideas for a bootstrapped business that can tackle that problem profitably and sustainably. All you need to do from here, is to keep going.

KEY TAKEAWAYS

o It's the community that leads you to the problem, which leads you to the product, which leads you to your business.

o Once you've found community-you fit, start contributing with the intention of becoming a pillar in that community.

o Pick the right problem (it's probably one you have), and confirm that others have it. Then confirm you have business-you fit too.

o When in doubt, always go back to the community. They will help you keep going and ultimately succeed.

Learn More

o Check out "1,000 True Fans," a blog post by Kevin Kelly.

o Read *Get Together*, a book by Bailey Richardson, Kai Elmer Sotto, and Kevin Huynh.

o Read "How We Gather," a report by Casper ter Kuile and Angie Thurston.

o Listen to Calendly's Tope Awotona on Guy Raz's *How I Built This* podcast.

o Follow Anne-Laure Le Cunff on Twitter (@anthilemoon). She runs a successful online community for makers, community builders, creators, and more.

3

build as little
as possible

Make **SOMETHING** people want.

—Y COMBINATOR

Make something **PEOPLE** want.

—ME

The previous chapter was all about finding a problem worth solving for people worth solving it for. In this chapter, I explain how to develop your idea and how to figure out what you need to do now versus what can wait until you're in business. Knowledge is important, but so is momentum. You don't want to get so in the weeds on which programming language to learn that you never start making your dream app. Especially at the beginning, minimalist entrepreneurs have to stick to what is truly essential rather than try to learn and do everything all at once.

While writers are often told to "write what you know," for entrepreneurs the process isn't so simple. When you're starting a business, you're often imagining something—a product, a service, a business model—that's never been done before. That said, most successful minimalist entrepreneurs have a solid background (or interest) in one aspect of the business they're starting even if they don't know everything about it or exactly how to begin.

For me, it was designing pretty, accessible software. When the iPhone App Store launched in 2008, I was one of its first wave of developers. Not because I was determined to start a business, but because I was following my passions and curiosity.

Unfortunately, in my conversations with aspiring founders, this moment is when most folks decide that building a business is not for them. They have the passion, but they let self-doubt creep in, convincing themselves that they don't possess the hard skills they think they need, such as iOS programming or financial modeling. Let me tell you a secret. Every founder, even the most successful ones, knows nothing at the beginning, and learns from there. This is about interests, not skills. Instead of focusing on the things you do not know, focus on the things you do.

You do not need a team, money, or a degree to start building. You don't need to ship or to code to make your idea come to life—*at first*. You might need them later, but when you are armed with a product that people truly value, these things will be easier and cheaper to acquire than you think. Often, they will find you. If your passion to solve a problem is genuine, you can overcome obstacles on your path one at a time. If you're on a mission to serve customers, you can learn what you need to know and delegate the rest. Just figure out where your skills, knowledge, and background intersect with the business you have in mind and leverage these strengths to the hilt. Don't get permission. Just get started.

Anna Gát, founder and CEO of Interintellect, was determined to build platforms where people could peacefully share their beliefs in spite of growing polarization in public intel-

lectual and political spaces. The first inkling of the idea had come to her between Brexit and the 2016 elections in the United States. Gát felt that a great cultural shift was happening, and she was eager to be part of creating the way the world would look in the years to come. It was a bold idea, but she had accomplished a similarly challenging task several years before as cofounder of Hungary's leading women's rights website and events community, for which she won a *Glamour* Woman of the Year Award. Now she was focused on creating mediated spaces that would allow people with irreconcilable opinions to come together. Her first iteration was a platform for academics where adversarial conversation and research could take place, but within a few months, she found working with that community to be a much slower process than she had anticipated. What she was building wasn't scalable.

Her second version of the product, a messaging app that would facilitate public discourse through artificial intelligence, was even more ambitious. For two years, she poured

all of her energy, money, and time into building a new platform, working nights and spending every dollar she had to
fund testing and development. Unfortunately, as the product
moved closer to launch, many people who had said they would
use the app were not as interested as they had indicated in
preliminary research.

"I was hell-bent on building technology," she says, and the
whole endeavor had been so expensive and time-consuming
that she was reluctant to abandon it. But in the meantime, she
was organizing in-person salons where people could share
their opinions and ideas. She didn't consider these gather-
ings to be a business, but she knew she had inadvertently
created the vibrant intellectual community she had been
seeking—it was just happening through the salons rather
than through the app.

Her entire career had been in tech, so building a company
with zero tech felt counterintuitive. She abandoned the app
anyway and pursued the "grander" idea based on the energy
and fun she felt in the salon community. Now Interintellect is
growing sustainably and realizing her initial dreams by way
of a low-tech, systematized solution that reflects what her
customers want and need.

Later in this chapter we'll talk more about Interintellect,
but I get why so many people start with software or technology when building a business. I love it too, but it's far too
constricting at the beginning of the creative process. It makes
the stakes too high, and it's too serious, expensive, and
stressful! That doesn't mean you shouldn't use engineering
strategies to get started. It's just that you don't have to jump
straight into coding or programming to create the processes
that will power your minimalist business.

The world will tell you to go big or go home, but I say go

small at the beginning. And the smallest you could possibly start is to build nothing at all. Instead of skipping straight to software, stick with pen and paper.

Start with Process

Every big idea was small first. If you don't start small, if you can't help people one by one, you will struggle to build a business around your idea. Leave your ego at the door, set aside your concerns about funding and software, and focus on your first customers, using your time and your expertise to solve real problems for real people.

Now that people know you, trust you, and perhaps even turn to you for expertise, it is time to start helping them in a systematic, repeatable way that allows for continuous improvement and iteration. As you fulfill the first customer cycle, document each part of the process so that with every consecutive customer you have a playbook. This document will be the true MVP of your business. I'm not talking about the minimum viable product that we're all trying to build and to launch. I'm talking about the *manual valuable process* that precedes it and will be the foundation for the business you're trying to build.

Methodically creating this manual valuable process and recording the steps you take to complete it will help you figure out what's working and what isn't. It will also help you discover if you're making something that people actually need or will buy. In his book *Anything You Want*, CD Baby founder Derek Sivers writes, "If you want to make a movie recommendation service, start by telling friends to call you for movie recommendations. When you find a movie your friends like, they buy you a drink. Keep track of what you recommended and how your friends liked it, and improve from there."

Unfortunately, the English language does not have a word for this activity, so I made one up:

processize *(verb)*

to turn into a process:
After they tested it on their friends, they processized their recommendation system.

It really should be a word in the dictionary because it is so important on the path to building a business the right way. Unfortunately, many people miss this step, falter, and ultimately fail because they go straight from problem to product before learning exactly what and how to build. But processizing is a cheap, quick discovery process that is essential. "Creating a product is a process of discovery, not mere implementation. Technology is applied science," Naval Ravikant says.

Without processization, you may think you know what the customer actually wants, maybe even because the customer has told you what they want, and maybe even what they would pay for. But as Anna Gát can tell us, talk is cheap. Until you get through the entire process of solving the customer's problem and (ultimately) receiving payment, you won't know what the customer wants and is willing to pay for. You need to solve one customer's problem reasonably well, if imperfectly, before you can scale. If it works, great. If it doesn't, you may realize *you* want to scale up, but your customers couldn't care less. If that's the case, you may want to consider a different idea.

One minimalist business built on process is Endcrawl.com. For eight years, founder John "Pliny" Eremic ran a post-production company for the film industry and watched filmmakers struggle to produce the end credits that listed all of the people, places, and organizations that appeared in or contributed to the making of a film. He and his cofounder, Alan Grow, knew there had to be a better way, and the obvious answer was some kind of software to manage the endless changes and updates that made the process so painful. But they didn't start there; instead, they set up a Google Sheet and a simple Perl script to build end credits to help them learn about their customers and validate some of their core assumptions. Their initial process looked like this:

o First, they gave customers a Google Sheet with their end credits formatted to their specifications.
o Customers could edit the Google Sheet as often and as much as they like.
o Once customers wanted a new "render" or video output of the credits, they emailed the request.
o Pliny or Alan manually exported their Google Sheet to CSV.
o Then they manually ran the CSV through the Perl script.
o Next, they manually uploaded the files to Dropbox.
o Finally, they manually emailed the customer the download link.

For filmmakers used to waiting up to twenty-four hours, it was a revelation that this process, even manually, took only about fifteen minutes. It also allowed the customers to control their data and to do an unlimited number of revisions for a fixed price until the credits were just right. For customers, life was just a little bit better. For Pliny and Alan, it was a chance for discovery.

Build Last

Even after you help your first few customers, you might not be totally sure how to solve the problem you have chosen to solve for your community, but one of the easiest ways to get started and to experiment is to freelance. Selling your time does not scale nearly as well as other types of businesses but can generate positive cash flow much sooner, giving you the breathing room to think about what comes next.

In my experience, many of the best minimalist businesses started out as freelance work or side projects before evolving into viable companies with potential for long-term growth. As you consider what exactly to build, there are a few routes

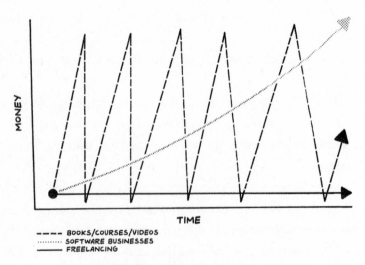

Forms of self-employment income for developers

that will get you to a profitable, sustainable business in the quickest, most efficient way. They are:

○ **Selling your knowledge and teaching people via digital content (videos, ebooks, podcasts, and courses).** Lynda .com, which LinkedIn acquired in 2015, grew from a book and a series of in-person workshops led by Lynda Weinman. When the dot-com bubble burst in 2001, Lynda and her husband, Bruce Heavin, offered a subscription service to the online educational videos they made about web design, an idea that was new at the time. At first it seemed that the business would not survive, but as Lynda.com's subscribers grew from just a few hundred to hundreds of thousands, their industry impact also expanded astronomically.

○ **Selling a physical product (merchandise or a unique product offering).** Noxgear manufactures light-up visibility vests for runners and cyclists. The idea first came to cofounders Tom Walters and Simon Curran when they patched together a version of what would eventually become the Tracer360 for their nighttime ultimate Frisbee games. When they looked into what was available in the marketplace for early-morning and late-night athletes, they saw an opportunity, prototyped their product, and sold the first five hundred vests on Kickstarter. They've since added the Lighthound, a light-up harness for dogs.

○ **Connecting people for a flat or percentage fee.** Craig Newmark started Craigslist as an email list among his friends, highlighting local events in the San Francisco Bay Area worth checking out. Today, they are doing over $1 billion in revenue per year, with fewer than a hundred employees. But while Craigslist is the quintessential example of connecting people, there are many ways to do this. Job boards, like People First Jobs (which we discuss in chapter 7 on culture and hiring), connect companies with candidates, often charging a flat fee for doing so. And there are communities too, like Product Manager HQ, that connect like-minded folks with each other.

○ **Software as a service (SaaS).** The idea of building a software solution that would optimize remote work and minimize distractions came to Justin Mitchell and his team at Yac in 2018. In four days, they built the first iteration of what would eventually become their asynchronous voice messaging app for Product Hunt's Makers Festival, because they saw a hole in the market for remote workers who were constantly dealing with the demands of Zoom meetings and the distraction of Slack. Although YAC's platform, integrations, and features have grown since then, it all began with the small idea of eliminating interruptions.

In the last chapter we covered the four different kinds of economic utility: place, form, time and possession. To come up with your offering, you'll likely overlay that list onto the list above to come up with the type of business that best solves the problem you're trying to solve for your customers. For example, you may save people time (time utility) learning a new skill with an online, cohort-based course (digital content). Or you may build software (form utility) that automates a manual, physical process (SaaS).

Over time, your business will likely offer two or more of these products and services, but at first, you should pick one to focus on and get started. In general, that should be the one that lets you begin today, instead of tomorrow.

Remember that you don't have to know everything about what you're doing at the beginning (or ever), and many people are wrong the first time about what they are building. The fact is, it's very likely that you discover the kind of business you should be building as you are building another business you thought you should be building. As Adam Wathan of Tailwind UI says, "Want to find a good SaaS idea? Start a business, literally any business. You will soon realize how bad every existing tool is that you have to pay for to run that business, and you will quickly become overwhelmed by the number of things you feel you need to build yourself."

If you make a false start, just go back, reset, and begin again. Nothing you've done or learned is ever wasted. A sustainable, growing business will take years to fully develop, and because you are growing as the business wishes you to, you have the time to make adjustments and learn the skills you need to know to succeed at each step. That's because you are not doing this the unicorn way, which the venture capitalist Marc Andreessen refers to as "baking a cake in three minutes." You are using your slow cooker to make a soup, on low heat and in full view.

And if you're not rushing, you have time to talk to customers, time to iterate, and time to test your hypothesis.

Test Your Hypothesis

A business hypothesis is just like the one you learned in fifth-grade science class. It is a suggested solution for a problem that does not currently have a solution. It must be testable (able to be tested repeatedly and independently) and falsifiable (able to be proved wrong).

For example: *My customers will pay a fixed fee with a small premium to get their end credits quickly and efficiently produced with as many renders as they need.*

Every business starts by testing a hypothesis with real customers. And if you only have one customer, you can treat your startup like a white-glove service. This may mean a phone call or sitting across the table from your customer at a local coffee shop, helping them with their problem.

The goal of these meetings is to validate this hypothesis. It takes time to test and honest reflection to recognize when you are wrong. But it is better to be wrong now, when the stakes are low, than to be wrong after you have spent five years and some of your own personal capital trying to build your idea into a business that was never meant to exist.

When you are validating a hypothesis, do not ask leading questions—questions that point people to the answer you want to hear. Instead, think about creating the kind of feedback loop that author and tech entrepreneur Rob Fitzpatrick writes about in *The Mom Test*. When you ask the kind of questions he recommends, the kind even your mom can't lie to you about, you will get the honest truth, because no one will know that you have a new idea for a business and that you're testing to see if it's viable. For example, you shouldn't ask:

Would you pay for my product?

Instead, ask:

Why haven't you been able to fix this already?

There are many businesses that cannot be proved in this way, but these are not the types of businesses we are interested in building. We're aiming to build businesses that are testable at a small scale, and can then be scaled up gradually, over time.

Another benefit of this approach: You can charge for it. If you are genuinely helping someone, you do not need to wait until you have a product to sell in order to make money. You can be paid for your time like Pliny and Alan were even before they technically had a "product."

In their case, the process they created proved their hypothesis that filmmakers would pay for a solution to the problem of trying to finish the credits. Your first idea may not go as smoothly, and that is totally okay—most experiments are wrong. You are at the frontier, literally trying to make something that does not exist yet, and you will be wrong a lot on the way to figuring out what your customers want. As long as you are working toward being right through processization, you only have to be right once.

And when you do arrive there, you will have a document that dictates your perfect process, because as you've walked someone through solving their problem, you've refined the steps it takes to get there. This process will take future

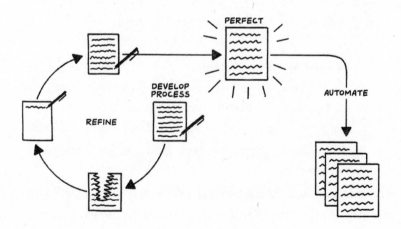

customers from nothing to something. It's something you can share (perhaps publish). You haven't made any money. You don't necessarily have a business *yet*. But you've provided what Paul Graham, the founder of Y Combinator among many other endeavors, calls a "quantum of utility: when there is at least some set of users who would be excited to hear about it, because they can now do something they couldn't do before."

Do One Thing Well

Before I launched into research or coding or brand building, I picked a single problem to solve for myself and for my community of creators: selling digital files to their audiences. The basic assumption was simple, that people were starting their careers on the internet, some of them finding enormous success through social media rather than with websites and blogs. But at the end of the day, when they needed a platform to sell what they were making, they still wanted somewhere to send people and a streamlined way to deliver digital files and get paid for them.

At its start, like any good product, Gumroad really only did one thing. The original Gumroad website reads:

1. **Take a file or a link of value.** This can be anything. From a link to an exclusive build of an app, to a secret blog post, to an icon you spent hours designing.
2. **Share it.** Just like any old link. Choose your own price. You don't have to create a store. And you don't have to do *any* management.
3. **Make money.** And that's it. At the end of each month we'll deposit the money you've earned to your PayPal account.

If you think building an app like that is insanely complicated, it may be useful to know that most apps on the internet
consist of two things: forms and lists. Twitter, for example,
has a form you use to tweet (with a single input) and a list of
tweets you see from people you follow.

These apps are referred to as CRUD apps, as they have
four actions you can take: Create, Read, Update, and Delete.
And Twitter doesn't even let you edit tweets!

Gumroad fit this model. At first, I let a creator create, edit,
and delete products, and allowed consumers to view them
("read" them). Stripe made payments easy to take, and Pay-
Pal made it easy for payouts to be sent out (albeit manually
at first).

Gumroad didn't have file uploading at the time (you had
to specify a destination URL post-purchase, like a YouTube
URL), and I didn't even have automated payouts or fee calcu-
lations. That was all manual.

The whole app was twenty-seven hundred lines of mostly
copy-pasted code in a single Python file, hosted on Google's
cloud. (I've since open-sourced the code; find the link at the
end of the chapter.) But it worked! It solved the problem. So I
launched. Of course, it wasn't "ready" for the masses, but ten
years later, Gumroad still doesn't feel ready. I don't think it
ever will be.

Wait a second, no payouts? Nope! Instead, I collected everyone's PayPal information. At the end of every month, I
made a list of everyone's email addresses and their account
balances, and paid everyone out one by one. Eventually, I
started to automate bits of it. Instead of copy-pasting lines
from the database, I wrote some code to download a list.
Later, I wrote a script that would issue the payouts using Pay-
Pal's API.

There were still issues. For example, whether you made a sale on August 1 or August 30, you would still be paid out on August 31, meaning fraudsters could make a bunch of sales a few minutes right before they're meant to be paid out, circumventing our ability to review and block the transactions. Since then we've added a seven-day buffer, though we got away with not having any buffer for at least a year or two.

Over time, we automated absolutely everything, which made all the difference when I needed to run the ship single-handedly. But we didn't start there! First, I "hired" myself to do it. Then I built a process around it. Then we turned parts of it into a product, now wholly automated.

What Should I Build?

To this day, processizing is a concept we employ over and over again at Gumroad. Everything I do is listed on a piece of paper that everyone in the company can access. When I go on vacation, someone else can take over my job. And if I get hit by a bus, the company doesn't go under. Once you have this magic piece of paper, you can turn your process into a product. We don't have to make up a new word for this because it already exists: "productizing."

Productizing simply means developing a process into something you can sell. In the processizing stage, you created a manual valuable process for yourself and built a system for working efficiently and effectively as you helped each individual customer. Now you are ready to productize, which means that you automate each individual task so that people can sign up, use, and pay for your product without you being involved.

If processizing is how you scale a manual process, then productizing is how you go fully automatic. Just like a brick-and-mortar business in your local community needs some essentials to get up and running, you will need to do the same for your minimalist business. And if you have to go back a few steps, don't worry, because that's part of the process too.

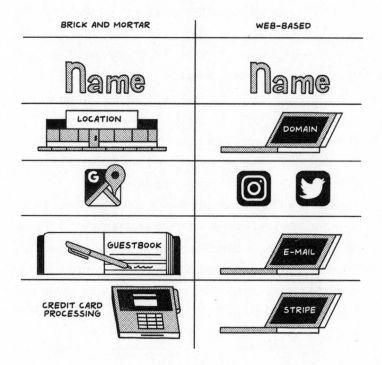

o **Name your business.** Before you can tell anyone about your product, you need a name. I like names that take two words and combine them, because I find them easier to remember than a new, made-up word. I also think they help with word of mouth because everyone will know how to spell them. This is also called a "radio test": If someone hears your business's name on the radio, can they find it using Google? Gumroad, Dropbox, and Facebook follow this model. But honestly, your name doesn't matter much. Take it from the founder of Gumroad. If you're successful, your name will feel right.

- **Build a website and create an email address.** The equivalent of your brick-and-mortar store is a website. To do that, you need to buy a domain; it will cost you about $10 (renewing yearly). Connect it to a website-building platform like Carrd, Gumroad, Wix, or something else. These will cost about $10 a month. Create an email address for yourself with that domain (sahil@gumroad.com, for example), as well as a password manager.
- **Create social media accounts.** You'll need two sets of accounts, one for you personally and one for your business (you'll see why in the chapter on marketing).
- **Make it easy for customers to pay.** Get a Square or Stripe account. These are payment processors that will help you collect credit card payments online and in person. They are free to sign up for and cost about 2.9 percent plus 30 cents per transaction. (You may want to spin up an LLC too, but I tend to wait until I have a few customers before committing.)

Now your business is ready to accept your first customer. If someone asks you what you are working on, you can give them a URL they can check out (if not checkout!). At the beginning, you should use it to explain what your product does and provide an email for folks who may be interested in such a thing, even if you do not have a product yet. You can and should always be learning and interacting with prospective customers.

Once you have these in place, you can start building. But what exactly to build? As little as you can. We'll get into launching in the next chapter, but this chapter is about building. That means you need to start shipping, and shipping means you should start with almost nothing, because the job is to start delivering value for your community/customers as quickly as possible. And they don't want to wait!

Constraints Lead to Creativity

If you're a minimalist entrepreneur, the early stages are all about constraints. Now that you're productizing, you have to add in more limits. In addition to your product doing just one thing (at first), there are other ways to control the temptation to try to do everything at once . . . or to try to do it perfectly.

I ask myself four questions every time I want to build something new:

1. *Can I ship it in a weekend?* The first iteration of most solutions can and should be prototyped in two to three days.
2. *Is it making my customers lives a little better?*
3. *Is a customer willing to pay me for it?* It's important for the business to be profitable from day one, so creating something valuable enough for people to pay for is key.
4. *Can I get feedback quickly?* Make sure that you're building a product for people who can let you know if you're doing a good job or not. The faster you get feedback, the faster you'll build something truly valuable and worth paying for.

Note that there are no constraints around how pretty the product is or how well written the code is. That's another reason to do as little as you possibly can: to be honest with yourself about how useful your product actually is. A product that is beautiful or has great marketing behind it may *feel* more useful than it actually *is*. But if your product is incredibly minimal *and* useful, and people look past the lack of polish and use it, you will know you are on to something.

The perfect example of this is Craigslist. It's never been pretty, but it's always worked so well that it didn't matter. And it's so useful that it's spawned a whole world of businesses created from that model. The goal here is to build something "good enough." Good enough to show others, and good enough for them to pay for. Which is almost always much less than you think.

Ryan Hoover launched Product Hunt, a site for product-loving enthusiasts to share and geek out over the latest mobile apps, websites, hardware projects, and tech creations, with an email list and Linkydink, a tool for creating collaborative daily email digests. It happened quickly. Hoover says, "Over Thanksgiving break, we designed and built Product Hunt.... [Five] days later, we had a very minimal but fully functional product. We emailed our supporters a link to Product Hunt, informing them not to share it publicly. The supporters were thrilled to join and play with a working version of something they had thought about and, indirectly, helped build. That day we acquired our first 30 users. By the end of the week, we had 100 users and felt ready to share Product Hunt with the world."

From the very beginning, Product Hunt had enough momentum that Hoover realized it was a project worth pursuing. His day job building tools for game developers had given him time and space to experiment (see freelancing), and he had a clear idea of what he wanted Product Hunt to be. He knew he didn't need to reinvent the wheel; he could use something similar to the format of Reddit. But since he wasn't an engineer, he still found himself asking, "How am I going to build it? Who will develop it?" In the end, rather than get bogged down by those questions, he decided that the newsletter was a superquick, no-code way to get the project off the ground and build some confidence around his idea.

Like me, Ryan doesn't believe that founders should start with code. "Do shitty work people love at first," he says. As more and more infrastructure gets built by new businesses (including, perhaps, the one you're working on now), it is getting cheaper, faster, and more accessible to build an MVP without code. What that means is that you shouldn't wait until tomorrow to get started. The lower the barriers to entry, the more competition you will have.

The trendline is simple: democratization. Everything that a software engineer can do today, everyone can do tomorrow. It means you need to know less to do more. Even if your service is manual, or your product is physical, you will be able to take advantage of software to provide your service as efficiently as possible. Every single business is in some way tech-enabled, even though the end product may not be.

For example, if you are building a software business, you can visit Makerpad.co and learn how to connect Gumroad and Carrd to accept orders on your website without writing a single line of code. And when you are ready to automate your manual fulfillment process, it will teach you how to add Airtable and Google Forms and Mailchimp. There are products like Notion, which we use to run our entire company. And there are services like Zapier, which allow you to automate the connections between all the software you use. Seriously, check out Makerpad. You'll be surprised how much you can build without writing a single line of code.

Similar to processizing your workflow as you were helping people, these tools will let you processize and later productize the internal functions of your business itself.

Perhaps most important, they will save you money. The further you can get without hiring your first engineer if you are building a software product, the higher your chances of achieving profitability. And the further you get, the better the employee you can hire. (And more often than you think, these people will find you!)

Ship Early and Often

Building a business is a lesson in fast feedback loops and iteration. Imagine if you were on a boat searching for treasure, but you could only ping your radar once a year. Then once a month. Then every day. The boat is your business, and the treasure is product-market fit.

You will be wrong a lot; the goal is to get less wrong as quickly as you can. This is why shipping early and often is so important. Gumroad, for example, has never shipped a "v2" in ten years. Instead, we have shipped tens of thousands (literally) of incremental and major improvements over time. Each time, we cross the threshold for some customer from "I may want this later" to "I need this now."

Your goal is to move away from being paid directly for your time. This is important because your time is far more valuable than your money, and so you should almost always welcome the trade. Over time, you can improve on the exchange rate, but you should always know what it is.

For example, if you are helping people for $10 an hour, you can set a goal to get to $20 an hour. You can do this by building software tools to help you do your job twice as fast, or you can increase demand for your service such that you are able to charge more. Ultimately, you will be able to make the equivalent of thousands of dollars per hour, but at the beginning you're still learning and iterating as fast as you can. After all, what matters is not just the processes you build for your business; it's also the processes you build for yourself.

While it may seem obvious how to productize a SaaS business, productizing isn't just about coding and software. It applies to any minimalist business, including Interintellect. Because Anna Gát processized early, Interintellect has a predictable, repeatable format based on four pillars: creating a moderated space, allowing equal speaking time for participants, promoting fun and entertainment, and establishing a patient, transparent, multidisciplinary atmosphere. The salons are organized and tracked by topic, time zone, and host, and a tight feedback loop allows the company to surface the most discussed topics in the community forum and to program events based on customer preferences.

"One interesting thing you only learn in practice after doing it a thousand times," she says, "is what you're really making. I was convinced I was making events at the start, but I'm really making hosts." As a result, Gát has launched a new platform that will enable hosts to build and schedule their own events and to approve, onboard, and train new hosts based on the incredibly strong set of norms by which the community abides.

As Interintellect expands, Anna expects to further automate the company's processes so that they can host sixty events per day around the world. For her, the goal of Interintellect salons is ultimately entertainment even as she systematizes a ritual around how people congregate so that they can learn, share, and interact in an intellectually relaxed space.

Even if your business doesn't at first seem to lend itself to processizing and productizing, Interintellect is a good example of how this methodology can be applied in almost any setting.

Create Conditions for Liftoff

At the end of the last chapter, I talked about squashing doubts, but if you're like 99 percent of the founders out there, doubts will be with you every step of the way, especially when you bring your product out to a community that you know and respect. Even though selling to strangers is inefficient, people are still desperate to avoid the awkwardness of telling their community what they're working on. Sorry, but it's still absolutely critical to start there.

This self-doubt never goes away. Even when you conquer community, you'll still have self-doubt about product. When you build and ship a product, you'll have self-doubt about sales. When you've done everything mentioned in this book, you'll have self-doubt about whether you're qualified enough to write it all down. (Hi!)

Just get going, and keep going. Your failures will fade, while your successes will stick around and compound. You didn't believe you'd get this far, yet the data shows that you did. Remind yourself of that as often as you need to, I certainly do.

We began this chapter talking about momentum. Let's finish talking about confidence: As you build the solution you'll sell to your first customer, you will also gain the confidence to know you're on the right track and take the next leap forward.

If you're lucky, you may be able to get away with building

almost nothing. If you've solved a true pain point for real people, they won't fault the simplicity of your offering but appreciate you for it. Some will even ask to pay. This is the exciting part: You made your first dollar on the internet. You crossed the great divide from zero to one. You started.

KEY TAKEAWAYS

o Refine a manual valuable process before building a minimum viable product.
o The faster the feedback loop you have with your customers, the faster you'll get to a solution they will pay for. The fastest feedback loop will be one you have with yourself.
o Before you build anything at all, see how little you can get away with charging for it. Even later, build only the things you need to build. Outsource the rest.
o I define "product-market fit" as having repeat customers who sign up and use your product on their own so that you can start to focus on outbound sales.

Learn More

o Read *Getting Real*, a free "book" about building a web app, by Basecamp, available online at https://basecamp.com /books/getting-real.
o Read *The Mom Test*, a book on how to talk—and listen—to customers, by Rob Fitzpatrick.

o Browse Gumroad's original source code, which I recently published online at https://github.com/gumroad
/gumroad-v1.

o Explore Rosieland, @rosie.land, a resource for community
builders created by Rosie Sherry.

o Follow Daniel Vassallo (@dvassallo) on Twitter. He made
a living on Gumroad before joining as our quarter-time
head of product.

4

sell to your first hundred customers

It just took off. A true viral success.

—NO ONE, EVER

After building a product, many people think the next step is launching it to the world. Hollywood has premiere parties, while Silicon Valley has Demo Days, Product Hunt launches, and "Show HN" posts.

This obsession with launching is not exclusive to Hollywood and Silicon Valley. It pervades the thinking of cities and towns throughout the world. There's probably a restaurant near you with a giant red sign pinned over its entrance reading GRAND OPENING.

It invites you in, with a promise that you'll be one of the first. Maybe you'll get a deal. But tomorrow, and even a month from now, the sign is still there. They're always opening, and grandly too!

Lots of businesses go this route. Jeffrey Katzenberg, co-founder and former CEO of Dreamworks, and Meg Whitman, former CEO of eBay, founded streaming video service Quibi,

a cautionary tale of launching before actually going to market. The company raised $1.8 billion and bought Super Bowl ads, expecting the whole world to flock to their service. It planned a launch party, meant to draw 150 celebrities among its 1,500 guests, that was canceled due to the COVID-19 pandemic.

Ultimately, the app bombed. Only 300,000 people downloaded Quibi on day one, compared with Disney+'s 4 million. One month post-launch, Quibi had fallen off the Top 100 chart, and within six months it shut down and returned its investors' money.

This experience isn't so different for software businesses. Two excitable cofounders work on an app, submit it to Product Hunt, and see thousands of sign-ups on the first day. A few months later, no one is using it, and they're on to a new project. Rinse and repeat. But businesses are not something you engage with once, talk to your friends about, and then forget as you move on to the next thing. Your business should have customers for life, not just for a Friday night.

That's because the real story of starting and then growing

a business isn't really that thrilling most days. Between start and success, it can be a slog. It can take years. And it often isn't nearly as glamorous as you expect. But you will have many small victories, and over time they will build into a sense of satisfaction and pride that comes from not giving up.

In the last chapter we focused on process and product, but once you have your MVP, it's time to turn your attention to your first customers. If you wait too long, if you endlessly iterate without showing your work to the world, you may feel productive even though you are slowly (or quickly) running out of runway.

That's why it's so important to start. Once you have enough repeat customers, you have product-market fit, which is a milestone worth celebrating and a sign you can think about launching. Until then, skip the one-time grand opening, and instead focus on the slow and steady journey of selling to your first hundred customers.

Sales Is Not a Four-Letter Word

I interviewed a lot of people for this book, and you wouldn't believe how hard it was to get anyone to talk about sales. No one likes the stereotype idea of selling—it's sleazy, and it depends on information asymmetry—but that is not what we are doing here. You already have a relationship with the community, and you're selling a product that adds value to the life of a customer who is happy to pay for it.

Eventually strangers will buy your product, but mostly because your customers are spreading the gospel of your business and product, not because they saw an ad. But it will take time to get there. It's not something you hit on day one.

Look at your own life: When was the last time you went on

Twitter or Facebook and shouted from your digital balcony about a product you loved? It just doesn't happen that often.

"Viral success" is a myth, pure and simple. There is no such thing. It's just something journalists say about a person, company, product, or service whose seemingly rapid rise is inexplicable from the outside. Most of us—and that includes journalists—only notice new things when they've reached escape velocity. We're often unaware of the previous months or years of hard work and stumbles.

At the end of this chapter, you will launch, but it's because you'll be celebrating milestones that will actually mean something about the longevity and sustainability of your business. You will be profitable, you will have customers paying for your product, and they will be telling other customers about it. Then you can launch—or rather, you can celebrate by saying thank you to the community and the customers who have helped you build from nothing to something.

Until then, treat the sales process as an opportunity for discovery. You think your product is market-ready. It's probably not. You think you've figured out the correct pricing tiers. You probably haven't.

Turn every failed conversion into an insight. Either you're talking to the wrong person and you need to shift your focus, or they're the right person but your product still has work to do to solve their problem. Both are good learnings, learnings you want to have before you start marketing to a broader audience.

For now, sales is an education process. Your customers will get to know you, and you'll get to know what's working, what's not, and how to fix it. Selling might not always go smoothly at the beginning, but I guarantee waiting won't make it any easier. Once you've figured out how to get started, the next challenge is pricing.

Charge Something, Anything

Pricing is hard. In the early days, you may be tempted to give your product away for free or to charge less than the value of your time or the raw materials you used. Don't. In order to stay alive, you need to make money. The only way to do that is not only to charge something, but to charge something that allows you to stay afloat. If you've productized, then you've already figured out an initial pricing structure for your first customers, and pricing, just like every other part of a business, is subject to iteration. Eventually, the type of customer you have will influence how and how much you charge, but at the beginning, as you build your solution, keep in mind that you're able to charge in two ways:

o **Cost-based** (things that have inherent costs—for example, web servers or an employee's time). If you need to pay a certain amount, you can add a "margin," say 20 percent, and charge that. For example, retail stores often buy wholesale and double the price when they sell it to consumers (giving them a margin of 50 percent). Marketplaces such as iTunes or iStockPhoto often go with this method.

o **Value-based** (a feature with clear value). This is charging for something not because it costs you money to deliver, but because it has inherent value for the customer. For example, Netflix may have a multiscreen feature that doesn't cost them any money to provide (beyond the engineering costs to ship the feature in the first place), but they are able to charge a monthly fee for it.

The goal is to eventually charge people for tiered levels of service, which you can do when your product, service, or software has an established value and brand. Think of the tiers as you would think of the different types of plane tickets—you'll get to your destination whether you sit in economy, business class, or first class, but with substantially different levels of service. Tiered pricing is a common practice for most software businesses, and it changes all the time depending on the features offered. For example, Circle.so, a community platform for creators, has three levels of service, basic, professional, and enterprise, based both on the number of members in the community and on available features and integrations.

Even if you start low and go up over time, it is important to charge something. There is a very large difference between free and one dollar—that's the *zero price effect*. As behavioral economist Dan Ariely writes in *Predictably Irrational*, "people will jump for something free even when it's something they don't want." He uses the example of a long line of college students waiting for free, terribly unhealthy brownies. Asked to pay even just one cent, the line of kids disappears.

(Later, you can consider introducing a free tier. This model, popularized by venture capitalist Fred Wilson, is often referred to as "freemium.")

Advertising-driven media models are another example. When the reader doesn't pay anything, it's often hard to convince them that it's valuable when the time comes to start charging for it.

Pricing decisions are not permanent. A price is just a part of a product, like everything else, and it can and will change

over time. Similar to product development, your goal is to start the discovery process, not get to the perfect result right away.

It's worth noting that when prices for products do change, they generally go up. This should be true for you as well: As your product improves and you are able to provide a better service, your offering will become more valuable to your customer as well—and you may even introduce higher tiers for your superusers.

Once you've picked a price, you need to shop it around. I recommend starting with those closest to you: your friends and family.

(Unfortunately, not everyone has a supportive family. Feel free to substitute a chosen family in its place.)

Friends and Family First

In Silicon Valley, there's a term for the first round of funding: the "friends and family" round. This may be even more common *outside* the Bay Area, where venture capitalists and angel investors do not patrol the streets looking for things to fund. But friends and family aren't just important when it comes to funding. Whether or not they've given you a dime up until now, it's worth pitching them to be your first customers.

This may make you uncomfortable even if you know that friends and family are in the dead center of your community. It certainly made me uncomfortable, shoving my business in my friends' faces and asking them to try Gumroad when I knew I didn't have all the kinks worked out yet. But when you're just getting started, with few credentials to your name, who trusts you more than your friends and family? And if they don't, who will?

Yet people believe they can skip their friends and family in favor of launching and going viral. For example, on Kickstarter. But even Kickstarter knows this isn't the case. "Millions of people visit Kickstarter every week, but support always begins with people you know," it reads on their website. "Friends, fans, and the communities you're a part of will likely be some of your earliest supporters, not to mention your biggest resources for spreading the word about your project."

Projects do go viral occasionally, I'm sure, but virtually none without a big initial push from the friends, family, and fans of the project's creators. All of that is to say it's normal and maybe even expected to rely on friends and family to provide initial support, and to be the first to buy your product. If you're having trouble with that, remind yourself you've built something you think provides real value. It's worth paying for even if it's not perfect!

PleaseNotes founder and CEO Cheryl Sutherland was using journaling and affirmations to uncover her next professional step when she came up with the idea for her company, which offers coaching programs and makes journals and other products geared toward personal development. A close friend who was a graphic designer helped design her website and her first product, the PleaseNotes, a set of three sticky notepads printed with affirmations. Two other friends who had a crowdfunding consulting business advised her on how to launch an effective Kickstarter campaign to generate preorders for her second product, a PleaseNotes journal. Her goal was to raise $10,000. She eventually raised $15,054 from 253 people, many of whom were friends and family. That money allowed her to test the market and gave her the momentum she needed to keep going.

That early proof of concept is invaluable. It takes time for a restaurant to figure out their menu, hence soft openings with friends and family. It takes time for a movie to figure out its pacing, hence test screenings. The same goes for your business and your product.

Once you've addressed feedback and turned your friends and family into customers because your product is genuinely good, you can move on from your friends and family, and into your communities.

Community, Community, Community

Over time, this becomes less about *you* and more about your *product*. Your friends and family, whom you started with,

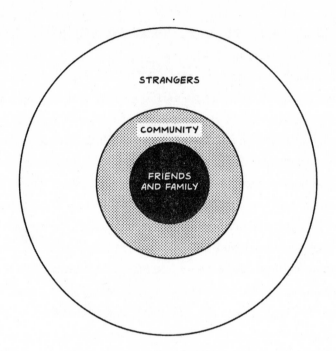

cared most about you. Your community cares less about you and more about your product.

This is the same way your business grows: starting with the people who care about you the most, and "ending" with the people who care about you the least.

Even if you've successfully solved a problem for your community, it may take some time and patience to get their attention. Humans, like objects, have inertia. Everyone is on a path, and it usually takes a bump to knock them in a different direction, even if it is a better one in the form of the solution you're offering with your business.

Beyond the other human beings you personally know or are connected to, you can seek out similar customers in the physical environment around you. Every neighborhood, street, and downtown is a community where people live together and

hang out. In thriving communities, there are local businesses, event venues, and block parties. This is where life
happens outside of the office and the home. Put a poster
on the wall of your favorite coffee shop and on telephone
poles.

In the next chapter we'll talk about formal marketing, but
long before you ever implement a more structured plan,
you can still take advantage of opportunities for strategic outreach. Every community has reporters and micro-influencers,
who cover the goings-on within the community. In Portland,
where I live now, there are dozens of Instagram and Twitter
accounts about every facet of the city. These are student, am-
ateur, and professional journalists. They live to write about
what you are up to.

This is how you make that happen:

1. **Make a list of everyone—yes, everyone—who has written or shared anything about a similar business.** A business launch. A business closure. A new product launch. A
   date night at that business. We can call these people *subject matter experts.*
2. **Contact them all personally.** Offer to walk them through
   your product, or meet them at your store, or give them a
   free meal. With Gumroad, I did this *literally* hundreds of
   times. And thousands of creators later, if I see a creator
   I really like whom I think Gumroad could help, I still reach
   out.
3. **Ask for their personal, candid feedback.** Do not ask for
   reviews, or a social media post, or for them to tell their
   friends. Your goal is to improve your product experience,
   and you should make it clear that you massively appreciate their support.

When you first bring your product to market, you may be part of one community, but that community will grow and change as your business grows and changes. It's simply discovering additional points of overlap and need and letting a broader group know that you have come up with a new solution to their problem. And hopefully, your customers will develop into their own community over time.

This is about building relationships. You will be doing business for a long time, and it is much easier to keep a customer than to find a new one. Never oversell. Be honest, open, and always kind. Show them how you most recently improved your product. Tell them a recent failing. Don't sell them on your product, educate them on your journey and learnings.

Cold Emails, Calls, and Messages

Long before you get to the bottom of the list of people you already know or could know, you're going to be sending a lot of emails, you're going to be making a lot of calls, and you're going to be knocking on a lot of doors. It's your job to reach out to friends, family, and members of your community whom you may not have seen for a while. Your calls are a chance to tell them what you're up to and ask them if they're interested in becoming customers. Some will say yes, but many will say no. Once you're okay with the nos, you're ready to sell to strangers.

In the early days (read: years) of Gumroad, we scoured the web for people who could benefit from a product like Gumroad and then told them about it. Literally thousands of times. That's the only way, really, when you're young and no one cares or knows who you are, to get folks to use your product.

Over time, you can get away with doing it less and less. But until you have a lot of customers or some other force that can supply ongoing momentum, there's nothing better than knocking on doors. This is a tried-and-true technique used by political canvassers, the LDS Church, and others . . . because it works! Trust me, if there was a better way, people would have found it.

Even Katrina Lake, CEO of Stitchfix and one of *Forbes*'s Richest Self-Made Women in 2020, started out with cold calls and cold messages on LinkedIn to potential investors. "The more shameless you can be, the thicker skin you have, the better," she says. "People are going to not write back and people are going to say no, but every now and then someone's gonna be interested and say yes. And you wouldn't have had that chance if you hadn't gotten all the no's first." While you may not be hitting up investors, you will be talking to people over and over again who will say no. The sooner you get used to it, the sooner you stop taking it personally and use those nos as a learning opportunity, the better.

I get it. It's awkward and uncomfortable to reach out to people you don't necessarily know personally, many of whom will ignore or reject you. My sense is that people who wish to reach customers some other way, like search engine optimization (SEO) or content marketing, are looking for an out. If that's you: Stop! It doesn't exist! Just hunker down and dedicate some time to finding people, reaching out to them personally via email, phone, whatever, and being okay with it sucking for a while. You may find that talking about your process and your product and the path you've taken to get there is far less difficult than you think. After all, this is your work, and if you're bringing it out to the world, you should be excited and proud, so don't skip this chance at discovery.

A stellar launch doesn't change this. Fanfare doesn't bring real customers, as Quibi learned. Consistent growth comes after a long period of time, mostly driven, especially at the beginning, by a hardworking sales team—starting with you.

If you need help getting started, here's an example:

> Hi John,
>
> I saw you're selling a PDF on your website using PayPal, and manually emailing everyone who buys the PDF. I built a service called Gumroad, which basically automates all of this. I'd love to show it to you, or you can check it out yourself: gumroad.com.
>
> Also happy to just share any learnings we see from creators in a little PDF we have. Let me know!
>
> Best,
> Sahil, founder and CEO of Gumroad

Don't copy-paste. Each email will refine your ability to write better emails. Done right, you're not only educating customers, but educating yourself about what you can do better. It's a learn-learn situation.

Manual "sales" will be 99 percent of your growth in the early days, and word of mouth will be 99 percent of your growth in the latter days. It's not a glamorous answer, but it's true. Things like paid marketing, SEO, and content marketing can come later, once you have a hundred customers, once you're profitable, and once your customers are referring more customers to you. Only then!

The best news of all is that once you have a hundred customers, you can use the same playbook to get to a thousand.

Once you have a thousand, you can use a similar playbook to get to ten thousand.

When Slack IPO'd in 2020 at a valuation of $16 billion, its offering documents showed that 575 of their customers accounted for approximately 40 percent of their revenue. This just goes to show that you need far fewer customers than you may think.

Big network-focused tech companies boast dazzling metrics, but their actual profits (when they have profits, anyway) come from a very tiny portion of their total audience. The rest of us might do better to ignore the lurkers and freeloaders altogether and focus on core customers. Depending on the nature of the product or service, anywhere from a few dozen to a few thousand regular customers will be more than enough to keep a business viable long-term.

Mailchimp is a good example of how focusing on smaller, reliable customers might make more sense than swinging for the fences. Ben Chestnut and Dan Kurzius first started a web design agency called the Rocket Science Group with a focus on big corporate clients, but at the same time they also built Mailchimp, an email marketing service for small businesses. For about seven years they ran both businesses, until they closed the web design agency in 2007 because they found that working for small businesses gave them the freedom to be more creative and adapt quickly to their customers' needs.

Chestnut and Kurzius have a universe of offerings, but Mailchimp's service is free up to the first two thousand emails. Once customers want to send to a larger list or need extra services, their plans begin at $10 per month and go up from there (see the earlier conversation on tiered pricing!). Even though

Mailchimp could broaden its reach to corporations or institutions, the company's customer base is still small businesses, and they've not strayed from their mission to build out features for their core community.

It may be surprising, but it is not a coincidence. Whether you're just starting or you've been in business for years, your most important clients are your community. They trust you because you've helped them grow their own businesses. It's not happenstance that they're ready to support you when you have your own.

This isn't just about huge SaaS businesses either. It applies to smaller businesses too. Across the spectrum of minimalist entrepreneurs, I see a common pattern: manual sales, finding your community, talking about your journey, highlighting your customers, and getting authentic coverage. If you started with community, and you continue to pay attention and solve the persistent problems your community has, then those first customers can take you very far.

Growth-at-all-costs is all about selling to strangers so that you can scale, but profitability-at-all-costs means you don't need to depend on strangers to keep your business afloat. Instead, you can rely on your existing customers from your communities and eventually from your audience. They'll spread the word as they feel comfortable doing so, and that's how you'll grow. The math looks different for everybody, but the goal is the same: financial independence. When I did it for myself, I needed about $2,000 a month to maintain my lifestyle.

If your product costs $10 a month, like Gumroad's, you need two hundred customers. That doesn't seem so bad. There are about 260 business days a year, so you'd get there in less than a year if you acquired one customer every business day.

Daniel Vassallo tweeted recently:

Daniel Vassallo @dvassallo · Dec 30, 2019 ...
2000 customers @ $39/month is almost $1M/year.

- You don't need to dominate the market.
- You don't need to disrupt anything.
- You don't need to conquer the competition.

You can add 1 new customer/day & before you know it, you'll have a $1M/yr machine. Wouldn't that be enough?

Q 144   ⇄ 1.2K   ♡ 7.6K   ⬆

That doesn't sound so hard, does it? You may already be selling a product for someone else for your day job. Sell your own!

Sell Like Jaime Schmidt

Jaime Schmidt never launched Schmidt's Naturals, a natural deodorant brand she founded in 2010. Instead, she celebrated small milestones along the way before eventually selling her company for more than $100 million in 2017 to Unilever.

When Jaime was pregnant with her son, she started a deep dive into the world of natural personal care products after taking a class in DIY shampoo. While there were hundreds of recipes available for soaps and lotions, there were few, if any, recipes for deodorants even though many people were concerned about ingredients in traditional formulations. Jaime had tried all of the natural deodorants but had found that none of them worked for her, so she decided to make one herself. She experimented for months until she found an effective formulation and landed on a scent, cedarwood, that she loved. Six months after the shampoo class, she had a product line of lotions and deodorant, and she was ready to sell to her first customers.

She set up a simple website and a Facebook page for her business where she posted articles and recipes. In the first few months, she sold her products on consignment at two small local goods stores in Portland and on her own at a few street fairs and farmer's markets around the city. People stopped at her booth to try the deodorant and lotions, and she found a rhythm to her conversations with prospective customers: asking them about the products they used; talking about her products and how she had tested them; and convincing people that her natural deodorant actually worked.

The following year, she decided to go all-in on her idea. She took two part-time positions with stores that sold Schmidt's, a decision that served a dual purpose. First, interacting with the clientele gave her a chance to gather customer insights about her own products and learn about the inner workings of retail. But just as important, the income from those gigs served as the seed money to get Schmidt's off the ground. The in-store customers as well as the people she continued to meet at festivals and fairs were most enthusiastic about the deodorant she made; many times, they returned to tell her how well it worked and to buy more. She says, "Early customer feedback allowed me to perfect my formula, determine future scents, and recognize where I was making the most impact." And once she had refined her deodorant, "customers gave me validation that my product worked astonishingly well, and they spread the word."

Schmidt started 2012 with new, modern packaging for the deodorant, which was designed to set it apart from the competition. She looked beyond the direct-to-consumer sales channels and the natural and wellness retailers that her competitors used almost exclusively; in 2015, she expanded into traditional grocery stores and pharmacies, which allowed her to reach more customers and to enable greater access to healthy natural products.

Her creativity, innovation, and hard work paid off. Schmidt earned appearances on Fox News and *The Today Show*; mentions on social media from celebrities and influencers; articles in national publications; and distribution on the shelves of Target and Walmart. Though it was bittersweet, Jaime realized that a larger company with more resources could bring her vision and mission to an even wider customer base, and she signed the deal with Unilever right before Christmas 2017.

Reflecting on her journey, she says, "When I'm asked about what made Schmidt's so successful, I often say that my customers were my business plan. It started when I listened to those at the farmer's market, and it continued through each step of growth. Staying hyper-tuned-in to my customers always guided and served me." Not sales. Not marketing. Customers, educating, and being educated.

Launch to Celebrate

A launch is a stepping-stone. A thing that happens when your business already has customers, is doing well, and is going to last. Many companies go out of business within the first year. Why make a big deal out of a business before you're sure it'll stick around? Instead, build a successful business and "launch" as a celebration of your success. Spend your business's profits on it, not your own money.

Better yet, celebrate your customers' success. I think celebrating a milestone is a great excuse to launch. What about having successfully sold to a hundred customers? Once you're running a growing, profitable business with a hundred customers who love you and whom you care about, you can celebrate them—by launching. Throw a party. Invite all of your customers and thank them for their ongoing support.

Do that, and you'll have customers lining up at your door. They'll be people you already know, and who know you. Some of them will bring their own friends and families and maybe even members of their own communities too.

They may even help promote your event before it happens because you've told them about it and they're excited about supporting you. Plus, they can actually speak to others about how great your product is and how much better it has made their life. Your customers may be even better salespeople than you are. Good—there's more of them than there are of you!

Or perhaps you decide you don't need to launch at all. That's fine too. But entrepreneurship can be lonely, and it can be a good excuse to rally—and reward—your community for helping you get this far.

Once you have a hundred customers, some of them now repeat customers, selling your product better than you can, you're ready to move on to the next chapter of your business: marketing.

KEY TAKEAWAYS

o Launches are alluring, but they are one-off events I wouldn't bet your business on. Instead, wait until you have a product with repeat, paying customers. Then launch by thanking them!

o Selling your product (or process) directly to customers may seem slow, but it is worthwhile. It will lead to a much better product because the sales process will be less about convincing and more about discovery.

o Start by selling to your family and friends before moving on to your communities and, finally, if at all, to total strangers. (The further away from you, the harder they will be to convince.)

Learn More

o Read *Predictably Irrational*, a book on human psychology and pricing, by Dan Ariely.

o Read *How to Win Friends and Influence People*, by Dale Carnegie, the best book I've ever read on "sales."

o Read about how important cold email–based sales were in Gumroad's early growth in this interview I did with Indie Hackers: www.indiehackers.com/interview/i-started -gumroad-as-a-weekend-project-and-now-it-s-making -350k-mo-4fc6cbc0e8.

5

market by being you

Marketing is really just about sharing your passion.

—MICHAEL HYATT

Congratulations! You have community, a product, and a hundred customers. That means you've arrived at product-market fit, which I define more specifically for minimalist businesses this way: repeat customers. Repeat customers mean that your business is able to persist without ongoing sales efforts so you can start to focus on scaling. First comes scaling your customer acquisition and sales strategy, then your company, then your ambition.

So where does *marketing* fit in?

Marketing is sales at scale. Remember that before we built a minimum viable product, we had a manual valuable process. And before you can have marketing, you need to sell to your first hundred customers; that's because sales is the process upon which you build marketing. While sales is outbound and one-by-one, marketing is inbound and about attracting hundreds of potential customers at a time. Sales got you to one hundred customers. Marketing will get you to thousands.

But do not confuse marketing with advertising. Ads cost money, and minimalist entrepreneurs only spend money when we absolutely have to. We do cover ads later in this chapter, because they are a part of marketing, but in true minimalist fashion, we'll start with the free stuff. Because it's only once you've learned enough from sales—like you did with the manual process for your product—that you're ready to spend money on marketing.

It's much better to start by spending time instead of money. Blog posts are free. Twitter, Instagram, YouTube, and Clubhouse are free too. Instead of spending money, let's start there, by building an audience.

The Power of an Audience

You started your business by tapping into a preexisting community, and now it's time to move on to building an audience. What's the difference?

While your community is a part of your audience, your audience is not a part of your community. Instead, an audience is a network of everyone you can reach when you have something to say.

That may include your followers on each social media platform, your business's followers, your email newsletter subscribers, the people who walk by your retail store window every day, and more. If you needed to tell as many people as possible that the world was ending in an hour, how many people would you be able to tell? That's your audience.

Selling allows you to test the waters with these new people because it forces you to leave your bubble and convince them one by one, improving your product along the way. Marketing is harder, because instead of going to your customers, you have to make them leave *their* bubbles and come to you. People have lives and things to do, and using your product today is unlikely to make an appearance on their priority lists.

But if you can figure out how to bring customers to you, you'll have a much easier time scaling your business on all fronts. Hiring becomes easier, sales becomes easier, growth becomes easier. Everything about building a business becomes easier when you have a group of people rooting for your success that grows larger by the day.

In the last chapter, I talked about selling to your first customers, a.k.a. your friends, family, and community, and in this chapter, we'll talk about what to do when you've reached out to everyone you already know. I'm not a big fan of selling to strangers, but I am a big fan of bringing strangers into your audience and eventually turning them into customers.

People do not go from being strangers to being customers in one step. They go from being strangers to being vaguely aware of your existence to slowly over time becoming fans, and finally to being customers and then repeat customers who help you spread the word.

Start with making fans.

Make Fans, Not Headlines

Think about a company you like. Can you name the founders? Can you imagine what their office looks like? Can you hear their voices in your head? I'd bet that for many companies, the answer is yes.

Why are you able to do this? Because you've read articles

about them and follow them on social media. You are much more likely to buy their products, if you haven't already.

Unfortunately, most founders are not comfortable putting themselves at the center of their company's story. But you need to. People don't care about companies, they care about other people. And you've built something from nothing. You love what you do. You don't need to share what you ate for lunch, but you should take your hard-earned learnings and share them with the world.

I've seen that no matter how successful they are, many founders still suffer from imposter syndrome. There's so much you don't know, and so many people more knowledgeable than you. There are bigger businesses than yours with more revenue, more employees, and more accolades.

That will always be true, and it doesn't matter. You have something to offer. And your existing customers care. They are paying you for your work, they're interested in how you think, and they want to know why you made certain decisions and how your product came to be. As you grow and iterate, your product will improve. You will garner more credibility and trust. And you will have learned so much that could benefit others. When you were engaging with your community and selling to your first one hundred customers, you were already doing this. You were personally connecting, with people, telling them your story, and listening to theirs.

Building an audience, the first step toward making fans, is having these conversations at scale.

The Minimalist Marketing Funnel

The journey of each customer will be different, but it always starts with someone having no idea who you are or what you're

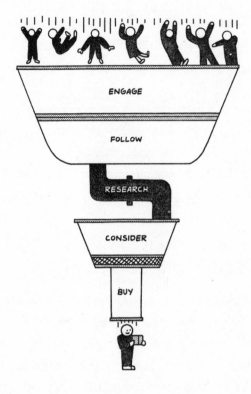

selling. Eventually, they will encounter your product somewhere in their Instagram feed or in a forum post or in a tweet
a friend shares. They will almost definitely forget about it.
One day, even though they'll forget who posted it, they may
"like" it. They may engage a few times.

Eventually, they will get interested—not in your product,
but in what you or your business has to say. They'll hit that
big "follow" button. Maybe they'll click through to your website and check it out. If they like what you think, what you say,
and how you say it, they may like what you've built too.

Most people will not be a fit for your business. That's okay.
Your audience will grow much larger than your customer
base—but your customer base is a subset, likely the most passionate, of your audience.

If they are a fit, they'll start to consider your product. Then signal their intent by signing up for an account, let's say, and then evaluating your functionality, pricing, and more. One day they'll purchase.

While you may be tempted to cut as many steps out of this funnel as possible, you may also want to add steps to it, like a free trial. But you can't shorten this process, no matter how much you'd like to. Every customer will engage, follow, research, consider, and finally buy (and hopefully buy again!).

Top of the Funnel: Social Media and SEO

There are eight billion strangers out there to have conversations with. Where do *you* begin? Start with the communities that your existing customers belong to, other than yours, and move outward from there. Marketing is second-degree sales, so your existing customers should *already* be spreading the word about your product. Ideally they're doing it because it makes their experience better. Your customers may go on first dates at your ice cream store, for example.

You can also incentivize this behavior. If you're an ice cream store, you may offer a free waffle cone to anyone who posts a story to their Instagram.

The analog world has the concept of "foot traffic." Real estate agents will tell you again and again, "Location, location, location." Location matters, because people are going about their day in the physical world, and if you happen to be where they are, literally, you may make a new sale you wouldn't have made otherwise.

Social media is not so different. Instead of Main Street, there's the Instagram "Explore" tab. Instead of Martin Luther

King Boulevard, it's the Twitter algorithm throwing new things you may appreciate (or be outraged by) into your feed.

These algorithms work by judging the theoretical "quality" of your content. The secret sauce is unique to each platform, but it is typically judged by what is going to lead to continued engagement by the end user. In general, this means that your content should lead to likes, shares, comments, and other forms of positive affirmation on the part of the consumer on the other side of the screen.

Location does still matter for digital products, just not in the same way that it does for the ice cream store. Just like you may choose a different mall for your storefront based on your kind of customer, your audience will live in different places online.

Twitter, to use one example, was a great place to start for Gumroad, because of the "retweet" functionality. It allowed our creators to share our tweets with their audiences. I've seen folks go from a few hundred followers to thousands because a single popular account retweeted their idea. And because it's often much easier to tweet than to produce the images, video, or audio necessary to post on other social networks, you can train yourself via a very quick feedback loop.

But it depends. Instagram may be the perfect platform for your business. Or YouTube, or Reddit, or Pinterest. Try them all. The good news is it's much cheaper and easier to try a new platform than to move your store to a new zip code. The world is in flux, and new platforms are constantly spinning up. You may find more success on TikTok, Clubhouse, Dispo, or something new that doesn't yet exist. The important thing is to start. Eventually you'll find the platform that will let you advertise your business by being you.

How to Get Started on Social Media

○ **Create an account.** One is your personal account (you, the human) and one is your business account (you, the business).

My accounts are my own (@shl) and Gumroad's (@gumroad). My personal account's goal is to encourage more people to start businesses. If you're reading this book, that's probably not surprising to you. Gumroad's goal is to inspire people to become creators, on Gumroad or otherwise. There's a subtle difference—creators and business owners are separate identities, but the fundamental questions are the same: Who is your audience, what do they want out of their life, and how can you help them achieve their goals?

Too many people think their business account is enough. No, it's not. People don't care about your business and its success, they care about you and your struggles.

○ **Don't share what you ate for lunch.** Status updates about your life and your business are fine, *but they won't grow your audience.* The days of discussing meals on social media are over, even on your personal account. Your goal now is to expand your reach and to provide the most value to strangers who find you on the internet.

○ **Be authentic.** Social media is about ideas, not people. Be yourself, but focus on acting out a set of core values. What did you learn? What conversation did you have? Your job here is to *give*, not *ask*. Remember: This is not about *selling*.

Your business account should be similar to your personal one, because they're both *you*, and both should be about ideas so that you're constantly giving value out for free. It may feel weird that you're not talking about a new customer case study or a new feature you've launched. You can do that too, occasionally. But the truth is, your audience doesn't care. They want to lose weight, laugh, be entertained, get smarter, spend time with loved ones, go home on time, sleep adequately, eat good food, be happy. Help them do that.

o **Build in public.** In chapter 2, I talked about community and sharing what you were learning in the process of becoming part of a like-minded group of people who share the same interests. Now it's time to take that a bit further on behalf of your business. Not only should you share what you learn to maintain your ties to your community, but you should also be building your business in public and sharing that process with your customers.

You don't have to be a genius or pretend to be a genius, you just need to be a step ahead of your audience in at least one thing.

o **Trust the feedback loop.** Start sharing, and you will soon find out what works and what doesn't. The brilliance of social media is the instant response (or lack of response) you get from your followers. As your audience grows, you will collect more data so that every day you can look back at what worked, what didn't work, and examine why. "Working" means something different for every business, but eventually your efforts should be quantifiable, objective, and should contribute in some way to your bottom line.

Just like your product, the stuff you share on social media is only as good as the experiences it enables people to have. This goes for Facebook, Instagram, YouTube, Reddit, Pinterest, and every other platform that connects like-minded people to each other. There are subtle differences, but you'll figure them out quickly as you go.

Soon, you'll be able to predict how something will land before you even say it. But since I've already gone through that, I'm here to help you out. I've learned that there are three levels to the type of content people share, each one with more potential reach than the last.

Educate, Inspire, and Entertain

It may be tempting to skip straight to the most "effective" type of content, but just like working out, you should walk before you run a 5K, and run a 5K before you run a marathon. Your body needs time to adapt, as does your mind. And most important, your audience does too.

Make your mistakes when few people are watching. The corollary of succeeding in public is failing in public, so you

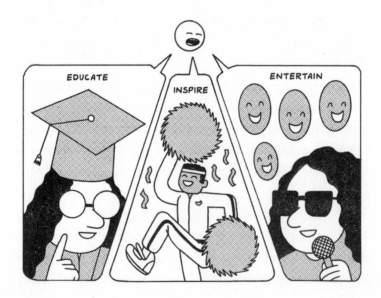

want the confidence and security of success at smaller scales before you move up the ladder.

LEVEL ONE: EDUCATE

Few make the transition from being themselves to being teachers, but those who do build audiences quickly, because people spend much of their time on social media in search of a better way to live, learn, and make money. This is how you start growing your audience beyond the people who already know you. You do it by providing value for free, asking for nothing in return, repeatedly. It's a natural continuation of what you were doing in your community, only now you're doing it with a wider group of people. If you have a hundred customers, there are at least a hundred things you have learned. Start by sharing those.

Your existing audience will engage with these ideas, broadcasting the very best ones to their own audiences, and yours will grow as a result. You will do this *every day*, because it's part of your job and because you're already online all day anyway.

Of course, this is not all you're doing. You're still building a company. Building a social media presence is a lagging indicator of the success of your company, and it should always be secondary to it.

In 2008, Jenny and Ron Doan lost most of their savings in the financial crisis. Their kids, Al and Sarah, came up with a plan to help get their parents back on their feet. They bought a computerized quilting machine to set up their mom, an avid quilter, in a small space in their hometown of Hamilton, Missouri. Al and Sarah hoped that given the demand and the long lead time for machine quilting, Jenny could take in other people's projects and finish them. If she could earn $10,000 per month, they figured, she could not only make a living, but could also rebuild the family's savings.

Business was so bad that their idea seemed dead on arrival. Al, who had already built several internet businesses, started looking around for a way to let people know about his mom even though he had no idea where quilters hung out on the web. What he discovered was that the internet had not yet touched quilting, and that most quilters closely guarded their techniques and designs in a way that kept people, especially beginners, out rather than inviting them in to learn, sew, and create.

Al persuaded Jenny to make ten YouTube tutorials in which she taught quilting techniques, and, well, the rest is history. Jenny's more than five hundred videos have been viewed millions of times, and in 2020, Missouri Star Quilt Company shipped more than one million orders. Hamilton has become "the Disneyland of Quilting," and the once-decaying small town hosts more than a hundred thousand people every year who come to visit Missouri Star's sixteen quilt shops, their restaurants, and their retreat center. All of that grew from ten YouTube videos.

If you're thinking, "I don't know where to start," or "Five hundred videos!?!," remind yourself that you've been practicing these skills for a while now. Remember how you participated in your community by commenting, contributing, and creating? You're basically doing that here at scale. It doesn't have to be polished, it doesn't have to be produced, it doesn't have to be perfect. The most important thing is to set aside a dedicated amount of time every day and to begin.

Education is a great way to get started, but to grow outside of your "students," you need to go beyond teaching. There are only so many people who are interested in learning physics, but Richard Feynman is much better known than any physics teacher would otherwise be because he talked about something grander than that. He took his insights from physics and turned them into insights about life. Technically his work falls into the category of philosophy.

At some point, he started motivating people, inspiring them to lead better lives. As physics became a subset of what he was teaching, his physics students became a subset of his new audience; far more people want to live better lives than want to learn physics.

How can you motivate and inspire? You can apply your learnings from painting, writing, designing, software engineering, or physics to life and share them with a wider audience. You can document your projects and your progress: where you started and where you are today. If you're in the supplements business, for example, a weight loss journey will gain far more traction than an information video.

Gimlet Media, a narrative podcasting company acquired by Spotify in 2019, launched its first podcast, *StartUp*, about its own humble beginnings. In the first season, founders Alex Blumberg and Matt Lieber tell the story of building their business, including one infamous episode in which Alex awkwardly and disastrously pitches venture investor Chris Sacca, who then shows him what his pitch *should* have been. Founder fights? Check. Burnout? Check. Family drama? Check. *StartUp* reveals some of the moments every founder faces but few like to discuss. The result? Millions of downloads.

Did the founders set out to inspire? Not necessarily. But by sharing their struggles and their successes, they showed others what was possible and made fans, not just customers. You can do the same. Don't just teach. Speak from experience, tell the truth, and the inspiration will happen.

LEVEL THREE: ENTERTAIN

This third level is the most important, because it makes you relevant to a vastly larger group of potential customers—almost everyone. But it is also the hardest to achieve.

Teaching is hard, inspiring is hard, entertaining is hard. Now try doing them all at the same time. Why? Think about how you spend your time. Do you spend it watching movies and TV shows and stand-up comedy specials, or—let's be honest—reading books like this one?

And even if you do read books like this, how often do you talk to your friends and family about them? It's more likely that you spend time discussing the last basketball game you watched, or the last political scandal, or the upcoming Holly-wood blockbuster.

When push comes to shove, entertainment wins.

Social media is no different. Every platform has a feed that puts all of the content head-to-head. There's one feed, for everything. If content is king, entertainment is the king of content.

You don't have to do something completely different. Keep educating people, and inspiring people, but have more fun doing it. You are still trying to teach people, but you want to do so in a way that sticks with them—and that happens when you make it entertaining.

Think about the three parts of a joke: (1) Say something, (2) establish a pattern, and (3) break the pattern with a punch line.

Here's one example that worked well for me. I often talk about entrepreneurship (big surprise!), but this tweet resonated and went viral . . . because it's funny:

Sahil ✔ @shl · Feb 10 · · ·

Entrepreneurship: work 60 hours a week so you don't have to work 40 hours a week.

💬 135   🔁 1K   ♡ 9.7K   ⬆️

You will fail at this, as I certainly have. Telling jokes is hard. And because it's the most subjective of the three, it will be harder to figure out why some things work while others don't. But that's exactly what building a brand is—the murky, "soft" stuff that isn't directly about the value you are creating for your customer.

Think about your favorite brands and how they communicate. Nike isn't selling shoes, and Apple isn't selling computers. They go straight for the heart, or the funny bone, and you should too.

But never forget: While social media is sexy and often leads to having millions of followers, it is not the end-all and be-all of your business. I've seen creators with tens of millions of followers fumble, and creators with just a few dozen earn a living multiple times over.

That's because social media is the top of the funnel. It's mostly strangers. Most of them are not fans yet, and almost none of them are customers.

You still need to convert them, and to do that, you need to get them to commit.

Middle of the Funnel: Emails and Communities

Don't call it a comeback. Email's been here since the very beginning of the internet. And it'll probably be here until its end.

Twitter, YouTube, Instagram, and Facebook can take away your business at any time, by tweaking the algorithms, shutting down your account, or making you pay to show up in people's feeds. So even though social media can be incredibly effective for gaining distribution, you are building on rented land.

That's why, as soon as you have social media followers, you should start building an email list.

Email is "peer-to-peer." It gives you a direct line to your customers that isn't controlled by a private company, an algorithm, or whether you spend money on advertising. And if you have someone's email address, it means they consider you a friend, not a stranger.

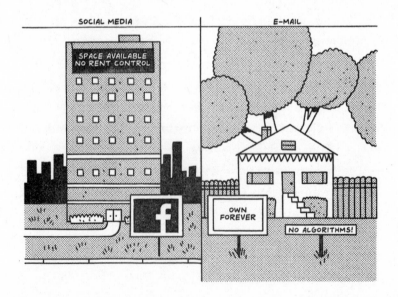

Of course, you don't spam your friends, so you shouldn't spam these people either. Apply the same three-level framework to emails as you do to any other type of content. First, educate. Second, inspire. Third, entertain. Ideally, you'll do all three.

Just like you built a process before you built a product, the earliest version of your email list may just be a spreadsheet that you update daily or weekly with the email addresses of your friends and family, your earliest customers, and the people in your community who have shown interest in your product. Eventually, you will want to automate parts of this process as your list grows and you have better uses for your time, like growing the list itself through sales, social media, and content.

To do that, you can use an email marketing service like Mailchimp or ConvertKit to collect emails from your most devout fans. To sweeten the deal, give them something in exchange for their email, like a mini ebook, a short PDF guide, a video, a series of emails that help them solve a problem, or a checklist to complete.

While you probably won't have millions of email subscribers, each subscriber is worth far more than a follower. Besides the product itself, Gumroad's email list is probably our most valuable business asset. More than 200,000 creators subscribe to the Gumroad newsletter. When we have something important to say—such as a new feature that will make our creators more money—we can tell all of them about it, without anyone else's permission.

(While we're here, subscribe to it: gumroad.com/gumroad/follow.)

Over the years, they've heard from us dozens of times, and they will continue to, until unsubscribe do us part.

You can encourage people to subscribe to your list in other ways too. In the previous section, we went in-depth on how to use social media. The next time you have a viral tweet, you can reply to it with a link to sign up to your newsletter. When you have something longer to say, write a blog post and link to that. At the bottom, let people know they can subscribe for further content. Go read your favorite blogger, and I bet you'll notice a form at the very end, with a free goodie on offer, often called a "lead magnet."

Finally, when you make a sale, virtually every service will allow you to ask for and collect your customer's email addresses, along with any other information you may want to ask for (such as their first name, or the city they live in).

Too many creators—trained by Amazon, perhaps, which doesn't give you any data on your customer—think of a sale as the end of a transaction, instead of the beginning of a relationship. The way we're marketing lets you build an audience of people who are hearing from you over and over again, before *and* after they've bought your product.

To get good at this, and for it to be most effective, you need to reach out to the people on your list frequently. Create a schedule, whether it's every Monday morning or every Saturday night or even just once a month. Pick something right now—you can always change your mind later.

The more consistent you are, the faster you'll find out what works for you. Not just the kind of content, but the platforms themselves. Your customers spend their time in different places, and you need to go find them.

You don't have to blog four times a week if a monthly newsletter with meaningful content is what you can manage and is more suited to your business. As with social media, experiment with how best to use your email list. If you send some-

YOUR SOCIAL CALENDAR	M	T	W	TH	F	S	S
🐦	X		X		X		
▶️			X				
📷					X		

thing out and readers unsubscribe en masse, don't do that again. But if you offer your knowledge, your insights, your experience, and a discount, and you see a response, do that over and over.

Eventually, your business will start to grow organically. You will no longer have to push that boulder up a hill. Social media algorithms will start to boost your content to new followers as you find your own success, your readers will share your blog posts with their friends, and your customers will start to tell others. How can you help them do so? By creating more content they want to share—that will help them educate, motivate, and entertain their own audiences.

How Laura Roeder Used Marketing to Grow

While I prioritize social media, other minimalist entrepreneurs like Laura Roeder, founder of Paperbell and MeetEdgar, have a different take. For Paperbell, a scheduling and client management software for personal coaches she founded in 2020, she decided on SEO-driven content marketing to engage her audience. Early on, she hired an SEO consultant to compile a spreadsheet of keywords that reflected the search intent of her target customers. At first she was worried that using SEO would compromise the quality of Paperbell's resources and advice for coaches, but instead it's helped focus her writing and has resulted in organic growth. "The amazing thing about SEO is that it's a long-term play," she says. "It only gets better over time if you put effort into it."

Though she does eventually hope to actively build up followers on Facebook and Instagram, right now she puts most of her energy into regular blog posts and product update emails, which she describes as her favorite marketing copy. All of the changes Paperbell makes to its software at this stage are in response to requests, so the update emails are a chance to delight customers who are invested in Paperbell's progress. "Founders put so much time into researching marketing strategies," she says, "but the only way to discover what will work is to try it, see if you like it, and watch to see if your customers respond." As the founder of multiple companies, she finds it freeing that there's no one right path for everyone and every business.

She knows because she's made changes between MeetEdgar and Paperbell. With MeetEdgar, a social media scheduling tool she founded in 2014, she and her team didn't offer trial subscriptions because the software required a time commitment to learn and to set up. But since then, there's been a behavioral shift in the way people research tools and consider software.

"Free trials are table stakes," she says. New customers aren't interested in marketing information; they open six tabs and want to get started comparing their choices right away. With MeetEdgar, she first tried invitations, but now both MeetEdgar and Paperbell offer trial subscriptions.

Laura is a big believer in building an email list from day one. Paperbell's list comes from her first customers as well as from those who've signed up for free trials. She also has a regularly changing lead magnet on the website to collect email addresses. The list is key because Paperbell is a low-cost software option for individuals rather than for teams, which means the math doesn't work to do demos or to have a dedicated sales team to reach customers.

"A lot of entrepreneurs think they have to start something totally new," she says, "but a proven market makes your job so much easier." With the way people buy on the internet, the quality and consistency of your marketing means that you can get on people's radar and you don't always need to create a unique product category to be successful against bigger companies. Instead, you can build great software and a great community into an impactful, sustainable business through patient, strategic, and consistent marketing.

Spend Money Last

Press cycles about million-dollar fund-raises and billion-dollar valuations are short-lived and targeted at aspiring entrepreneurs, not people like your customers. Building your audience that way doesn't work, because a months-old startup has nothing to say, besides that a few rich people gave them some money. Trust me, I know.

Most growth you see is paid for. So if you are jealous of someone's constant press and stratospheric growth, keep in mind that they are likely burning cash in order to acquire

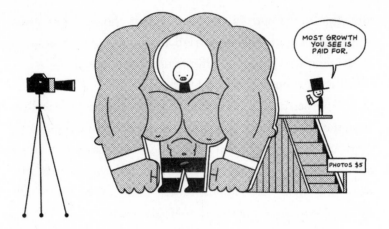

customers and to promise them an experience or a product that could come to an abrupt end at any moment when the money runs out. It is quite literally growth at all costs.

This is backwards. You started your business to help a group of people you care about, and your product is what you offer them, not your ad creatives. But it is too easy to fall for that trap when these are the examples that get the spotlight. Your product is not for everyone, so you shouldn't try to reach everyone. That's way too expensive. And if you're spending money to get followers, to get customers, or to get eyeballs on your product, you're buying an ad no matter what it's called.

There are display ads, social media ads, ads in newspapers and magazines, outdoor advertising ads, ads on the radio and on podcasts, direct mail, video ads, product placement, event marketing, influencer marketing, email marketing, and more.

This is an expensive set of rabbit holes to go down, which is why it's important to wait as long as you can before doing so. Ideally, you should have a clear idea of what's already working. Then, and only then, should you spend money to accelerate.

The stories about your business will be stories about your struggles, your customers, your learnings, and your journey. They will create more fans. Who will in turn become your customers, who in turn will tell others about your business.

There's another reason to figure out how to grow using your time and the customer base you currently have. Relying on advertising, even if it works for you today, may eventually get too expensive. The COVID-19 pandemic accelerated the move from traditional to digital advertising across all industries, which in the long run will drive the cost of ads up year over year. Just as you don't want to rely on social media companies to mediate your relationships to your customers, you don't want your business model to depend on outside companies providing you with affordable advertising. The sooner your marketing function is as sustainable as the rest of your business, the better. And there's no better time to start than from the very beginning.

Spend Money on Your Customers

Startups like PayPal and Uber spent millions of dollars in their early days paying their users to help them grow. But this may pose an obstacle to real growth. If people are only sharing your product because they are being financially rewarded for it, it is unsustainable.

Instead of thinking about loyalty programs as a marketing function, think of them as genuine rewards to loyal customers. For example, you can offer discounts for leaving a business review online or for sharing it on social media.

Eventually, you can worry about getting headlines from

journalists, but for now you should focus on getting reviews from your actual customers. Once your business is growing and sustainable, you can go beyond outreach to the community reporters and micro-influencers that I mentioned in chapter 4. Now you're ready to offer your product for free to reviewers and more established influencers, or you can offer samples of your products or exclusive information on your company to bloggers and journalists who cover your space. But most of all, you can just tell your story. You can be yourself. You worked hard for this. You struggled. You can show others that their hard work and struggles will be rewarded too.

Helena Hambrecht, cofounder and co-CEO of Haus, an aperitif brand, sees enormous potential in enlisting your best customers as marketers. This is one of the strategies she and her husband, Woody, a third-generation winemaker, are using to market their natural, lower-alcohol-by-volume spirits that they sell direct to consumer.

She and Woody didn't have money to put into paid marketing and customer acquisition, so from the first product launch at Haus, she reached out to her communities and pitched stories to the press and to individual influencers whom she knew would be excited by the company story and the content she posts on social media, including some of her own photography.

Given budgetary constraints, it would have been impossible for Haus to generate *all* the content they need for social media, and that's why Helena believes in "putting the power in customers' hands." Haus relies on user-generated content to generate word of mouth. Lo-fi content shot on an iPhone and genuine customer voices convey the authenticity that is a hallmark of the brand and that speaks to potential new customers.

The key, she says, is to build relationships, to make contributors feel valued, and to give them the tools they need to make content that they can not only use for Haus but that they themselves will be proud of. "Marketing doesn't have to be fancy to be impactful," she says. "It has to be real." Though Haus does spend money on ads, she notes that advertising performs best when it's surrounded by a lot of organic content.

She and I and many others believe that this is the only way paid marketing makes sense. Ads are anything openly sponsored and nonpersonal that are used to sell an idea, a political candidate, a business, or a product. The bad news is that we still live in a world in which huge corporations spend thousands or millions of dollars to reach thousands or millions of people, and entrepreneurs are up against the sophisticated marketing departments and advertising agencies of Disney, Coca-Cola, Nike, and the like.

Though technology hasn't completely leveled the playing field, it's made advertising a much fairer fight. There are more places to buy ads, with smaller audiences. And the more targeted you can get, the less you have to spend. This is good news for small businesses that don't have the large ad budgets of Fortune 500 companies and VC-funded startups but do have committed, well-defined communities.

You can advertise on Yelp, or Instagram, picking a specific geographic location or only people interested in, say, the oil paintings of John Singer Sargent. If you're selling a painting course about how to paint the human figure like an impressionist at the turn of the twentieth century, this can be incredibly effective.

A lot of people interested in those things will still not be interested in buying your product or service. A lot of people who like ice cream won't buy your ice cream. They may be dairy-free, or only eat ice cream on date nights, or they may like looking at ice cream more than they wish to actually eat it. Or perhaps they used to eat ice cream every day and now they're repenting for it. Who knows? You certainly don't.

But somebody (spoiler: Facebook) does. You don't need a whole marketing department, you just need a Facebook account. With their help, you can compete with the world's largest brands in just a few hours a week.

Take Advantage of Lookalike Audiences

I've already talked about the idea that the scale at which you can be successful with advertising is shrinking every day, thanks to software and the internet. As you browse, services like Facebook and Google collect data on your habits. They know what you need, want, and like. They may even be able to predict what you'll need, want, and like *tomorrow*. For better or worse, this is no longer surprising.

Collecting and using customer data is a strategy that's here to stay, but it inevitably leads to questions about internet privacy. From the outset, I've said that minimalist entrepreneurs should be selling *to* their users, not selling their users. In practice, that means building a product that solves a real problem for your customers, only selling to customers who are already convinced by your product, and only using your email list to send important information (not spam) to people who have opted in.

The same logic applies to ads. If you choose to spend money on advertising, you should do it in a way your customers would be happy about. As a bonus, you'll be able to spend less money to reach each new customer.

At Gumroad we don't spend any money on paid customer acquisition, for three reasons: (1) We can reach out to creators directly; (2) their use of Gumroad makes their own communities aware of Gumroad for us; and (3) I'm happy with our current growth rate. But paid ads can be a valuable tool for other entrepreneurs, such as ones selling high-quality consumer goods. That said, you should be mindful of the very real data privacy concerns users will have when they are on the receiving end of targeted ads. Ultimately, you have to decide if paid customer acquisition is the right fit for you and your business.

If you do decide to spend money, you will be glad that you waited. That's because you'll have a much better idea of who your customer actually is, and therefore who else may fit their profile.

For example, you can ask—and pay—Facebook if they happen to know folks who closely resemble your customers. These are called "lookalike audiences," which Facebook describes as "a way to reach new people who are likely to be interested in your business because they're similar to your best existing customers."

Instead of buying ads to target large swathes of the population, wasting their attention and your money, you can instead tell Facebook, "Please tell people who most resemble my existing customers that I exist."

Each company has its own name for this kind of ad. For example, Pinterest calls them "actalike." If you decide to spend money on this at all, it's a good way to get started. But remember that this kind of targeted advertising is also becoming

more expensive over time, possibly rendering a previously sustainable business unsustainable.

I could go on and on. There are a million different ways to advertise. But you should rarely, if ever, *need* to. A business built primarily through organic growth will be durable from the start, but even more durable over time as the businesses that heavily rely on paid advertising start to struggle.

Instead of spending money, spend your time. Build relationships, have passionate customers who spread the word, and then think about spending a little bit of your profits to slightly expand your horizon. If you can do that, you will stay lean and grow at a comfortable rate that never overextends your business.

But paid marketing should never get in the way of what really matters: talking to and selling to customers.

Bottom of the Funnel: Sales

Ultimately, this is what marketing is all about: selling to customers, at scale. Good news: You already have a ton of experience doing that.

That's why this part of the funnel is short and sweet. You've already done the hard work of building a product, finding initial customers, and making sure you've solved their problem. Now you get to revel in the fruits of your labor as your marketing starts to do the much more scalable work of attracting your next customers to you.

KEY TAKEAWAYS

o Marketing is not about making headlines, but making fans.
o Start by educating, then inspiring, then entertaining. Each of these three levels of content is more far-reaching than the last.
o Paid advertising can work, but it has its cons. If you do decide to spend money, wait as long as you can—you'll know much more about who you're trying to reach that way.

Learn More

o Read *Guerilla Marketing*, a book by Jay Conrad Levinson.

o Read *Made to Stick*, a book by Chip Heath and Dan Heath.

o Watch a video course by Daniel Vassallo.

o Look at room.club/tips, a guide I wrote on how to build an audience on Clubhouse.

6

grow yourself and your business mindfully

Life is like riding a bicycle. To keep your balance you must keep moving.

—ALBERT EINSTEIN

In this chapter, we're going to talk about what comes after you're profitable and have an organically growing customer base. For some of you, this will be relevant right this second, but even if you're not there yet, don't skip over this part. It will save you a lot of heartbreak if you can start thinking now about how to grow sustainably while avoiding some of the most common mistakes founders make.

You may be earning a nice living for yourself and your family, and in theory, your journey and the journey of your company could be coming to a close. But for many, including me, the point is not to create a lifestyle business, retire on a beach somewhere, and be done with it. The reasons to grow are different for every founder. Even though I got comfortable with the non-unicorn outcome for Gumroad in 2019, I've continued to invest in its growth. For one, it's fun and satisfying to work on a continuously improving project. Two, it feels good to find new ways to create value for our creators.

And frankly, staying put doesn't work. The world is constantly changing, and we and our businesses have to change with it. Staying put is a great way to start going backwards. You don't need to grow like crazy, but you also don't want to grow stagnant.

I've seen this play out at many companies. They solve the problem, get complacent, and over the years their customers churn and the people they hire are no longer fired up. But being a minimalist entrepreneur isn't just about owning a business that doesn't own you; it's also about owning a business that you want to work on, even if you don't *have* to work on it anymore.

At this stage, the real question is: How can I grow with intent, without jeopardizing the impact I make for my customers or damaging the life I've built? On the surface, it might seem straightforward to stay the course when you start to see results, but slow, sustained growth is its own kind of challenge that requires deliberate, conscious decision making.

When businesses fail, it's unlikely that a tornado of unforeseeable misfortunes is the cause. Instead, it's usually one or more of the same handful of mistakes: overspending on inventory and office space, hiring too quickly, cofounder infighting. I'll talk about how to avoid those mistakes, but also about how to deal with them because it's likely that some of them will happen to you, even if you try to avoid them.

There are two categories of self-inflicted mistakes, or "unforced errors," to watch out for. The first set relates to running out of money, and the second set to running out of energy.

Let's start with some basic economics and go from there.

Don't Spend Money You Don't Have

The most important equation in business: profit equals revenue minus costs.

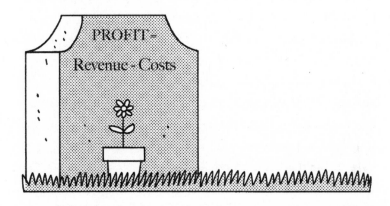

It sounds so simple: Make more than you spend, and your company can keep on going forever. Make less than you spend, and you will eventually fail.

But you'd be surprised how often founders ignore profitability (read: sustainability) and focus on product development, growing, hiring, and all kinds of other things, right up until the money runs out. Paul Graham, founder of Y Combinator, can size up a company immediately based on whether they're "default alive or default dead." If expenses and revenues stay constant, will the company live or die? Incredibly, half of the founders he talks to have no idea.

In Graham's experience, the founders don't know because they don't think they need to know. They're counting on investors to swoop in and save them if things go south. But if you're bootstrapping your company, *you* have to watch your own balance sheet because there's no one coming to save you from your own mistakes.

Let me state the obvious. You should already have revenue coming in from the hundred customers you sold to, plus however many you have acquired via the marketing methods I covered in the previous chapter. So if you're profitable now, you should be able to keep it that way by focusing on the only part of the equation left to discuss: costs.

There are two kinds of costs. The first is variable cost, also referred to as the "cost of goods sold," or COGS: the cost associated with selling each marginal unit of product. In brick-and-mortar businesses, that includes costs like labor, packaging, raw materials, and more. For software businesses in the 1990s, COGS were non-zero because software was put onto CDs and sold in retail stores.

Things have changed a lot since then. "Shipping" some electrons over the internet is virtually free, and the internet makes it much cheaper to collect payments online. For example, for each dollar we earn at Gumroad, we incur about 40 cents of variable costs. This 40 percent consists of payment processing fees, web hosting costs, other infrastructure costs, and fraud prevention (a necessary evil of helping people transact online).

That leaves us 60 cents per dollar. But that 60 cents isn't pure profit—we still need to pay the second kind of costs, fixed costs, which don't scale linearly with our revenue and each incremental product sold. This includes everything from our domain name to certain online services, but these aren't the main expenditures for us or for most businesses, minimalist or not. The number one fixed cost is people.

In the next chapter, we'll talk more about what it means to bring human beings into your company, but for now, let's just say that employees, their equipment, the office space they need, the internet connection, the insurance for the space,

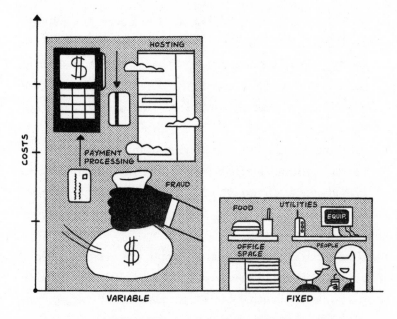

the snacks in the fridge, the electricity, and so on, cost a lot of money, and rightfully so. Starting with you, so . . .

○ **Pay yourself as little as possible, at least to start.** You are a founder, but you are also the first employee. Treat yourself as such. Don't expect to take dividends. Instead, pay yourself an annual salary even if it is just $1, and then increase it over time as you can afford to. This will force you to do the work to get your systems set up so you can have an accurate picture of how much or how little is required to run your business, not just sell your product.

If you're worried about making a living, I get it. That's why I've recommended again and again that you start your business as a side project and use your time, energy, and ideas to grow the business to profitability before you leave your day job. Then, you can pay yourself as profits allow. In my case, when Gumroad started to work, I paid myself $36K a year, just enough to cover basic living expenses in San Francisco. Over the years, I increased my salary but tied it to the salary of the lowest-paid person at the company: $60K, then $85K. When things went sideways in 2015, I paid myself $0 for a while. Now I pay myself $120K a year.

Ultimately, you should be trying to minimize your business's burn, but also remember that the goal here is to provide yourself enough of an income to be able to focus on what matters: helping your customers solve their problems.

o **Hire software, not humans.** People are expensive. Software is not, usually because a lot of it is VC-subsidized in the name of growth. Take advantage of this by using Pilot or Bench instead of hiring an accountant or a CFO. Use Gusto to run payroll and benefits in five minutes. Because you are putting off hiring, you will also save money on all of the people-managing roles in your company, like an HR person and an office manager (see below). You may be surprised how far you can get with cheap software tools. For example, you can hire a human being to follow up with new customers every time someone signs up for your service *or* you can use automation tools like Zapier to send a follow-up email and to add those new customers to a queue to call later.

o **Don't get an office.** I believed this pre-pandemic, and I, and millions of other people who weren't already convinced, believe it now. An office creates an insane amount of associated costs. Plus, you now have to manage an office. Unless you really need one, avoid it. (You can get one later if you really want it as a reward for building a meaningful, sustainable business.)

Thanks to the pandemic, there's a list of businesses a mile long that have become "digital by default," as Shopify founder and CEO Tobi Lutke put it, but others, like Upwork, have always thrived with distributed teams. Either way, even giants like Google, Microsoft, Morgan Stanley, JPMorgan, Capital One, Zillow, Slack, Amazon, PayPal, Salesforce, and other major companies have extended their work-from-home options post-2020, so if they don't need an office, you probably don't either.

- **Don't move to Silicon Valley.** Even before 2020, I would have said, "Don't quit your job, don't move to SF, don't pass go, and don't collect $200 (from VCs)." After all, San Francisco is expensive, traffic-heavy, and not a great place to raise your children—or even a dog. Now, post-COVID, remote work is the new normal, and that means you can stay where you are. Sam Altman, the former CEO of Y Combinator, said that he was "very excited to see SF have to compete with other cities." Me too. Not only is it cheaper and less competitive to build your company in a smaller town or city, but it's also better for the local community, which as we've learned can pay dividends for your business.

- **Outsource everything.** It's all you, every day. For now. Then it's software. Eventually you and your army of robots will be at maximum capacity and you'll need help. But before you hire your first full-time employee, use freelancers. I'm not talking about exploiting good, hardworking people by paying them less than they deserve. I mean hiring future founders and other potential minimalist entrepreneurs: offering them opportunities to learn within a functional, profitable business; paying them well; and giving them a chance to earn money while spending the rest of their time as they like—maybe even starting their own minimalist businesses themselves.

If you can use these tactics to keep your costs lower than your revenues, your business shouldn't die. Even better, you'll have something worth keeping: a profitable, sustainable, growing business serving customers. It's no longer up to the market to decide if what you built was valuable. It's now up to you not to lose it.

(This may seem overwhelming. To help, in the "Learn More" resources at the end of this chapter, I included Gumroad's *actual* P&L with all of our costs, as well as simpler examples.)

In the last chapter, I described how the Doans used YouTube to grow the Missouri Star Quilt Company from a struggling mom-and-pop machine quilting shop to a global quilting empire. Looking back, the success of Missouri Star might feel like a foregone conclusion, but it wasn't obvious at the start that the company would succeed, or even survive. "It took four years before we were profitable and could begin to pay our own salaries," Al Doan said. "We were doing everything ourselves, including renovating the buildings we bought, as we slowly figured out what worked both for our customers and for the company itself."

The good news for Missouri Star was that in Hamilton, Missouri, it was much easier to keep costs lower than it would have been in Silicon Valley or another market with expensive labor and real estate. "We started with a five-thousand-square-foot store that we thought would last us forever," Al said, but they eventually had to separate the company's inventory into multiple shops where they could house specialized fabrics, notions, and trim. As Missouri Star expanded, the "retail warehousing model"—in which the people who worked in the physical stores also fulfilled online orders—started to break down as employees could no longer simultaneously handle in-person and online sales.

The solution was obvious but also scary: To meet customer demand, Missouri Star would have to separate its retail business from its online one, which meant new warehouses, increased inventory, and more employees. As minimalist entrepreneurs, Al and his family were concerned about a radical increase in the company's variable costs, but because Missouri Star was already profitable and its revenues were growing year-over-year, they had the confidence (and the money) to support their expansion.

Al also had enough experience to know that avoiding growth and trying to maintain dysfunctional systems wasn't a good idea. "We didn't hire a human resources person until we were at 150 employees," he said, because it felt wasteful to pay someone to perform a function he'd done for years, "even if [he'd] done it badly." It took a few incidents and some intervention from a friend with an HR background for him to realize that investing in HR would be worth the cost. "Otherwise," he says, "you end up with several eight-hour jobs."

Beyond what the business has meant for the Doan family, Missouri Star Quilt Company has transformed the small town where it's headquartered. When asked about the impact on the community in 2019, Jenny Doan said that at first, "I thought we were just sewing," but now they employ four hundred people. In addition to growing Missouri Star, they've also started a sewing company, a knitting company, and an art company. "We have more ideas than we have buildings at this point," Jenny says.

The Doans' story offers many different lessons for minimalist entrepreneurs. Even if it's the goal, growth is its own challenge. Far too often, companies with plenty of talent and market potential run into trouble not because of the product or the customers but because of the unglamorous but essential parts of running the business: Operations. Finances. Human Resources. Legal. In the world of VC, where millions of dollars are thrown around on wild bets, people tend to be over-exuberant, lavishing generous perks like pool tables and free food.

Don't get swept up in what a "successful" business is supposed to look like. Keep doing what's working, stop or improve the processes that aren't, and always, always, always keep an eye on the numbers and your ears on your customers.

Stay Focused on What Your Customers Want

The tuning fork you should resort to over and over again is quite simple: your customers.

Your customers do not want you to get bigger and grow faster. They do not care how rich you are, if you were on the *Forbes* "30 Under 30" list, which venture capitalists you raised money from, or how many employees you have. They want your product to improve, and your business to stick around. That's about it.

Amazon has a nice way of thinking about this: "In every board meeting in Amazon HQ stands an empty chair. That seat represents the customer and the customer voice. So everything that is developed and created is scrutinized by the voice of the customer. That voice is what the people in the meeting room ask as if they were in the place and shoes of the customer. Why is this product important for me, what value does it bring, do we really need this service or product?"

Even though we're not trying to build Amazons, this attitude is even more important if you are at the helm of a newly profitable and growing minimalist business. As an African American father of six children, Jelani Memory, founder of Circle Media and A Kids Book About, inevitably found himself discussing racism at the table with his blended family of four white and two brown kids. Memory decided to write a book for his own children, one that would describe his experience with racism in terms they could understand.

The book, *A Kids Book About Racism*, was simple, with no illustrations. He proudly designed and printed one copy; it took four weeks to produce. It gave him a jumping-off point for discussing hard things with his own children, and when he showed it proudly to other friends and parents, many wanted a copy for their families. Even though he was in the midst of raising Series B for Circle Media, the idea of starting a publishing company had taken hold of him. By January 2019, he negotiated an exit.

At that point, he started to tell everyone he knew about his ideas for A Kids Book About—these were his potential early customers, after all—and seeing their reactions and feeling "the power of possibility in the look on people's faces" not only helped him refine the business but also validated his bigger project of publishing kids' books on challenging, empowering topics.

That energy kept him going through early challenges, including learning about publishing in general and figuring out how to manage inventory. He launched A Kids Book About in October 2019 with twelve titles, and it grew steadily but modestly until May 2020. The day after George Floyd was killed by police on May 25, 2020, "A Kids Book About did as much in sales as it had the whole previous month. And it didn't slow down," Memory said. "The following day, sales went up 2x, and the day after, went up another 2x and held steady. So, within the span of 10 days, A Kids Book About saw north of $1 million in revenue." Their inventory was supposed to last the rest of the year, but they sold out of every single one of their titles but two.

Those sales figures validated Memory's belief in the product he was offering and in the possibility for growth within a changing world. He says, "There is a misconception that money or investment confers validation and permission to do things in conventional and expensive ways, but that's not true. It's about product, revenue, and traction. Most of all, customer affection is the permission you need to grow."

If you stay focused on what drives sales and what excites your customers, then you'll know how to grow; they'll tell you. And if you pay attention as you go, even as you do unwittingly make unforced errors, it will be your customers (or the lack thereof) who will show you how to get back on track, far before you would have otherwise noticed.

Finally, be diligent about the essentials. It's easy to excuse sloppy practices when you're growing and feel overwhelmed, but that's the moment when you need to be most disciplined about how you spend your time and money. Not just because of the implications for your bottom line but also because nothing brings a business to a screeching halt faster than a legal problem or a break in the supply chain.

Paychecks need to go out on time, and it's on you to avoid any legal, financial, or operational complications that might sink the ship. Vendors need to be registered in the system and paid promptly. IT security needs to be buttoned up tight, particularly around user privacy. You need to run a good, clean business to establish and uphold your reputation with employees, vendors, and customers. Chances are, however, that one or more of these areas lies outside your area of experience. You probably lack even the basic knowledge to hire the right help. That's okay. We'll talk more on hiring in the next chapter.

Until then, good news: Your customers can connect you to people who can help, especially if you're open with them about what you need. They're already incentivized to support you, because they use your product and want to make it better. And there's another way to get them even more involved with your success: turning them into owners.

Raise Money from Your Community

Growing businesses, even minimalist businesses, may need capital at some point. Raising money can make sense, once you know how you would spend it to improve the lives of the customers you already have. Shopify, for example, and 1Password raised money several years into their lives. Because they were both profitable when they did it, they were able to keep their visions aligned and their dilution low, and retain control of their companies.

If you do choose to go the venture capital route (Hit me up! shl.vc), profitability will give you leverage in those negotiations. But there are also new ways to raise money, ones that preserve your ownership and empower your customers.

I don't just mean new venture capital funds such as Calm

Company Fund (disclosure: I am an investor), and Tinyseed Fund, which are looking to invest in more sustainable, perhaps minimalist, businesses. These firms are building a portfolio with a higher hit rate, allowing them not to overoptimize for finding the single company that returns their whole fund. But they are far from the norm.

What I am mostly talking about here is a totally new way to raise money from your customers and your communities: Regulation Crowdfunding.

In 2012, President Obama signed the JOBS Act into law. This bill, among many other things, included the ability for private companies like Gumroad to sell shares to the general public, making it possible for almost anyone to invest in the business. On March 15, 2021, the legal limit for regulation crowdfunding went from $1.07 million to $5 million. These new rules also allow for "testing the waters," allowing companies like Gumroad to see how much demand there is to invest in the company before committing to a crowdfunding campaign.

I believe that crowdfunding will reorganize the funding landscape. There will always be a place for venture capitalists, but who better to fund a business than its customers, who understand how valuable its offering is? And once founders can vet demand before committing, we should see the numbers skyrocket.

In the old way, the number one downside of raising money was that you created two distinct sets of stakeholders: your investors and your customers. This new practice will allow entrepreneurs to minimize complexity by turning customers into investors. All of a sudden, you have a single group of people you are serving: your community.

I can speak from experience: On March 15, 2021, I used

Regulation Crowdfunding to allow some of Gumroad's creators to become part-owners. In 12 hours, we raised $5 million from more than 7,000 individual investors. Now we have thousands of our creators as our investors too, keeping our interests more cleanly aligned.

For the businesses that neither need to bootstrap completely nor want to go the venture-backed path, I'm hopeful that Regulation Crowdfunding will offer a middle ground. But the ultimate long-term goal remains profitability (read: sustainability). Once you're in control of your destiny, you should never let it go.

Build Profitable Confidence

I know I've said over and over again that profitability is the metric that matters most to your business. That's because profitability is a superpower. If you rely on VCs for capital, like we did in the early days, you rely on outside forces to be successful. When they pull the plug, you have no more electricity. Your backup generator will last a certain amount of time, then run out too.

Profitability gets you off the grid, allowing you to grow mindfully with unlimited runway. You can take your time and make thoughtful decisions that move you toward the right targets at your pace, not someone else's. As some Navy SEALs say, "Slow is smooth and smooth is fast."

Chris Savage, CEO and cofounder of Wistia, a video and podcast marketing platform, calls the resulting sense of conviction "profitable confidence." In 2017, Savage and his cofounder, Brendan Schwartz, realized that their efforts to scale and grow quickly had not only made their work less creatively interesting, but had also made them unprofitable. By slowing down, they figured out how to trust their instincts again—and wound up more profitable than ever.

For Wistia, being profitably confident means that Chris and Brendan know they will live no matter what they do. It allows them to pursue ideas at their own pace, and that frees them up so that every single thing doesn't have to work immediately (or even at all). They don't have to bet the company anymore if they want to try something new, and they can wait years for something to pay off.

This feels great, because you can truly invest in the stuff that you think will create a lot of value for your customers, not just the stuff that will "move the needle" on your top-line growth metrics as soon as possible, so that you can raise the venture capital you need to keep going.

When you are profitable, you can take your time. You can talk to customers and really make sure you understand their problems before you attempt to solve them. Then you can iterate on your solution over and over again until you're really happy with it even if you take years to do it. You could even show customers and get their feedback again and again, like we often do.

Since you are running on your own steam, your runway will now last you forever. You will not die unless you do something stupid. This means you need to hire slowly, not ambitiously. You should also avoid irreversible decisions like getting a multiyear office lease. Moving slowly will mean you can ship more thoughtfully because you'll have the time and space to learn about yourself, your customers, and your market. It will also give you a clear view of the road ahead. You will be able to detect bugs in your product and systems before they affect your customers. You can test your software in private beta with customers, or behind a waitlist. You can make sure it's good enough before you give it a wide release. This way, your customers continue to appreciate every thoughtful addition—or subtraction—you make and to love your product without worrying about the mistakes that accompany quick changes and rash decisions.

Overcommunicate with Your Cofounder

Once your business is too well run to fail, there's one more failure point to address: you. Your business won't run out of money, but you may still run out of energy.

One of the fastest ways to drain your enthusiasm and to lose steam is a cofounder fight. According to Paul Graham, founder disagreements are par for the course, and 20 percent of those situations escalate until one founder departs the company.

No one gets married expecting to divorce, and most co-founders don't anticipate that things won't work out either. But ultimately, relationships are relationships, and it can be useful to apply frameworks for personal relationships to professional ones if they apply.

Drs. John and Julie Gottman, well-known couples therapists, say they can predict the end of relationships using "The Four Horsemen of the Apocalypse," their name for four types of communication styles that start to appear in a relationship: (1) criticism, (2) contempt, (3) defensiveness, and (4) stonewalling. While some founders succeed at tackling their conflicts head-on and eventually rediscover common purpose and mission, others never do, and one founder will move on.

CRITICISM

CONTEMPT

DEFENSIVENESS

STONEWALLING

In Startupland, this isn't necessarily a bad thing. Startups are encouraged to "fail fast," and founders often cycle through several teams at the same time they're cycling through ideas.

But there's also a lot of truth when people say, "It's harder to divorce your cofounder than your spouse," so if you want to give your business the best chance at success, approach the relationship with your cofounder(s) like a marriage. Think about the following before you team up for the long haul:

o Do not start a relationship with someone unless you really, really trust them.
o Do introduce vesting so that each of you earns your stock over several years.
o Do make sure you are aligned on your values, what you want to build, and how you want to build it.
o Do not ignore the possibility that one of you may leave. Plan for what a successful exit from the business may look like.
o Do have the hard conversations as early as you possibly can. Just like there's no point in dating someone for five years before you figure out if *they* want what *you* want, early in any serious professional relationship, it is important to explore and understand each other's values and ambitions. Because hard conversations get harder the longer you wait to have them. Here are some questions worth asking your potential partners:

   o *What does a happy relationship look like?*
   o *What does success for this business look like?*
   o *What does an exit look like?*
   o *How fast do we want to grow?*
   o *Why are we starting this together?*

Have these hard conversations again and again. Think about specific check-ins to reevaluate these goals so that disagreements don't fester silently, and make sure that whatever path you plan on taking, you're on the same page about it.

Maintain Your Energy and Sanity

The conventional wisdom is that there are two kinds of startup founders: On one end of the spectrum, you run a lifestyle business and lounge on the beach all day, and at the other, you work 24/7, only stopping to eat or sleep when absolutely necessary and sacrificing exercise, rest, family, the outdoors, and whatever in your life gives you pleasure and sustenance.

There's a lot of real estate between those two extremes, and just like your business needs to change and to grow to keep from getting stagnant, so do you as a human being. I'd be lying if I said that being a minimalist entrepreneur doesn't take a lot of hard work, but it doesn't have to be an all-or-nothing proposition.

I can speak from experience, as I've changed my mind about what I wanted out of Gumroad quite a few times. For the first several years of Gumroad's life, I was chasing unicorns. Then I right-sized the business to profitability, and today it's one of a few things I am working on, like this book. Generally, I don't let my business make me too happy, so that it can't make me too sad. But it took years for me to get here, and the kind of people who wanted to work on Gumroad at each phase were very different. I basically had to rebuild the whole team from scratch.

When you're growing at all costs, it's easy to avoid these conversations. It's easy to justify not having them too: You're all focused on growth, and these conversations aren't helping you grow in the short term. But in the long term, as your business morphs like every business does, you need to have them. Or they'll happen to you when you least expect them to, and that's a lot less fun.

To be clear, this isn't about scaling back your ambitions in order to make your business work. It's about aligning the ambitions you have for yourself and your company with the ambitions your customers have for themselves. Because I'm not trying to build a billion-dollar business at all costs, my focus now is on creating more creators and business owners.

And frankly, you often can't grow faster if you try. I've worked sixty hours a week for years on end, and I've worked four hours a week. For better or worse, Gumroad grew at its own pace, and the number of hours I worked didn't seem to have much of a correlation. I think you'll find the same is true for you: Your company will grow as quickly as your customers determine it will grow. For us, that was 15 percent in 2017, 25 percent in 2018, 40 percent in 2019, and 87 percent year-over-year in 2020.

It taught me to be wary of thinking I always needed to do more, earn more, or grow more than I needed to. Once I came to terms with the reality that I couldn't control everything, it got a lot easier to move forward. Instead of pretending to be a product visionary and trying to build a billion-dollar company, as if it were within my control, I could focus on making Gumroad better for our existing creators.

Some say that you need to grow like crazy, because "if you don't get big, someone else will eat you." As if companies were fish.

This is wrong. The vast majority of small businesses are never eaten. Big fish want to eat other big fish. In fact, the longest-lived businesses in the world are also some of the smallest. They are restaurants, hotels, construction companies, and more. Many of them are family firms, or small to midsize enterprises content with steady evolution of their niche and a passionate multigenerational customer base. Something to aspire to!

Maybe you already know this. Maybe that's the business you already aspire to build. If so, I'm glad. But it wasn't obvious to me when I started out, and I see these ideologies pervade and persist in social media, within headlines, and on TV.

One more economics lesson to wrap up: There's no free lunch. Once you have it, you will feel the pressure to spend money more loosely. Keep in mind the lessons we covered in this chapter as you start to spend your customers' money, making sure you're treating it as if it were your own. Instead of hiring like crazy, hire when it hurts. Instead of getting a fancy office, work out of a fancy coffee shop. When you do spend money, see how it affects your burn rate and your runway.

At this point, you know how to keep things going and growing. You're ready to start hiring and building operational excellence within your company to scale up. That's what we'll cover in the next chapter.

KEY TAKEAWAYS

○ Seek "profitable confidence": Infinite runway will maximize your creativity, clarity, and control. This is simple (spend less than you make) but not easy.

○ How to spend less: Do less. Don't move too fast, don't move to Silicon Valley, don't get an office, don't get too big. Grow as fast as your customers want you to—and are paying you to.

○ If you raise money, think about raising it from your community and turning your customers into owners.

○ Ultimately, most founders run out of energy before they run out of money. Maintain your energy and sanity, and that of your cofounders and coworkers, by realigning early and often on what really matters.

Learn More

○ Follow Chris Savage, cofounder and CEO of Wistia, on Twitter (@chrissavage), and read his post on profitable confidence here: https://wistia.com/learn/culture/profitable -confidence-how-to-build-a-business-for-the-long-term.

○ Read about "The Four Horsemen" by the Gottmans, starting here: www.gottman.com/blog/the-four-horsemen -recognizing-criticism-contempt-defensiveness-and -stonewalling/.

○ Check out the Gumroad crowdfunding campaign here: https://republic.co/gumroad.

7

build the house you want to live in

You can dream, create, design and build the
most wonderful place in the world . . . but it
requires people to make the dream a reality.

—WALT DISNEY

Whenever I have to decide what to do next, I ask myself the question Gary Keller poses in *The One Thing*: "What's the one thing you can do such that by doing it everything else will be easier or unnecessary?"

That's why in this book we've focused on community before process, process before product, sales before marketing, and marketing before growth.

When it comes to the people in your company, the answer to Keller's question is to focus on culture before hiring. Before you're ready to hire anyone, you first need to make a company people want to work for. That begins with setting your values, preferably as early as possible, because values are the foundation of the culture you will build together with your employees.

I used to think that communicating company values was kind of dumb, to be honest. Be nice, work hard, show up on time—isn't it obvious? Then I started Gumroad and realized that if you don't constantly remind everyone—including yourself—what you do, how you do it, and why you do it that way, you will veer off course. And then you'll have to make corrections, usually at the most inopportune time.

For me this happened in the fall of 2014, when I first started having conversations with VCs about the next round of funding for Gumroad. When I realized that it wasn't going to be easy, if at all possible, to raise our Series B round of funding, I had to realign several team members around a very different kind of culture—one focused on building a profitable, sustainable business rather than a unicorn. We didn't shift our priorities—we were and still are creators first—but our new focus required me to have conversations around the career trajectory some of our employees expected. And let me tell you, it's a lot more difficult, emotional, and expensive to fix your culture than your code.

Humans are not computers. We are all unpredictable, emotional creatures. Each person you hire makes the matrix of interactions within your organization more complex. You will make mistakes, but your company values will give you a plan of attack for how to get back on track.

Today, forty-eight people work on Gumroad, based all over the world, and they seem quite happy! But I had my fair share of ups and downs to get here. In this chapter, I'll share everything I've learned the hard way about hiring the right people at the right pace and keeping them happy and productive in the face of a never-ending barrage of lucrative and glamorous offers for their talent, particularly in the technology space. I also address the challenges and opportunities of remote work and other unconventional approaches to solving problems with people. It's an ongoing process that never really stops.

Before you invite anyone over, you need to get your house in order. I've never seen a house party end cleaner than when it started, and a company is a house party that never ends. So let's get started figuring out what kind of house you want to live in and then filling it with the awesome people who are going to come along with you on this journey.

Define Your Values Early and Often

Values are not generic two-word commandments that companies use to state the obvious. Quite the opposite: They're for stating the non-obvious, in non-obvious ways. They codify what you believe, putting it in a place where everyone can see—and everyone can suggest changes.

Values are oral tradition. They tell employees a story of how to behave in both everyday *and* extreme situations. And they're more efficient mediums of information than manuals and handbooks. That's because good values stick in the brain; they're efficient and memorable.

Nordstrom, for example, is famed for its customer service. In one iconic story, a customer brings a set of tires to the store to return even though Nordstrom sells clothes, not tires. The store accepts the tires anyway and fully refunds the customer. In another tale, a clerk who can't find the right pair of shoes at any nearby Nordstrom store recommends a competitor, Macy's, and covers shipping for the customer.

These stories communicate more about the kind of service Nordstrom—and its customers—expect than a thousand-page manual on "how to be a good sales clerk" ever could. You could start working there tomorrow and already have a good sense of what kind of standards you would need to uphold to be a good "fit."

That's because values aren't just for the people within the company. They tell your customers and the people who may consider working for you that you exist, and that they might be a great match. More important, they tell everyone else that your company isn't right for them, saving you, and them, precious time.

That absolute clarity is particularly important for minimalist entrepreneurs because we often attract people for whom this may be a first job. Defining and communicating your company's values early sets expectations for how work is done and how disagreements are handled within the organization. They're not just a vehicle for you to push your will on your team. They help hold your team together and provide a way for your team to hold *you* accountable.

Values supersede you, and values allow you to scale. After all, one of the reasons you started a business is to control your environment: when you work, how you work, where you work, who you work with, who you work for, and more. Values make sure that everyone is aligned on what that looks like. This is especially important when it comes to making difficult decisions.

Natalie Nagale, cofounder and CEO of Wildbit, knows this firsthand. She and her husband, Chris, founded Wildbit in 2000, and in 2012 the growth of Beanstalk, the workflow software that was one of their core products, plateaued.

"That was an important time for us," she says, "because we were forced to ask why we were building and what we wanted to grow." One of Wildbit's principles is that businesses are product agnostic, which helped them make the decision to shift Beanstalk to maintenance and support mode. When they finally stopped trying "to put out Beanstalk fires," they were able to focus on intentionally growing Postmark, an email delivery service that was their other core product.

In the years since, not being defined by one project or product has given Wildbit more freedom to "celebrate every opportunity to learn," which is one of their core values. In practice, this means that if something, even a long-term project, stops being interesting or challenging, they move on. After five years, Wildbit shut down Conveyor, meant to be a successor to Beanstalk, in 2020; this might have been devastating for another company, but for Wildbit it made space for their team to launch two new projects, People First Jobs, a job board, and DMARC Digests, a monitoring service to prevent email scams.

Making decisions that affect the lives of your team and your customers is not something to be taken lightly. But if you've decided on your values and have developed a culture around them, it will be a lot easier. A lot of founders think they can wait to write down their values, that they'll appear to them just in time, and that culture will develop naturally. That's true, but be forewarned that it may not be a culture you want for you, your team, or your customers.

You can start small and grow from there. But it is important to start having these conversations—even if it's just with yourself. You can communicate your values through pithy statements, or you can draw them out into long stories, but you should start.

At Gumroad our values exist in a culture doc titled "What Matters." And to help you get started with your own, I've embedded them for your reference below. They may not be exactly the right values for your company, but I hope they're a good starting point for reflection and action.

At this point you are already familiar with Gumroad, the product. Introducing … Gumroad, the company!

JUDGED BY THE WORK

This value is about being real about what matters: the experience creators—and their customers—have when they use Gumroad.

How I communicate this internally:

> Our creators don't care about us. They care about the product, content, and community we happen to provide. That means a few things:
>
> o While we often work in silos, we do not ship alone. Everything we send to creators is of the highest quality, meaning that *everything* is reviewed by multiple people on the Gumroad team, our creators (they're first!), and other folks in our broader community. For example, I published my Work article (sahillavingia.com/work) after addressing 600 comments from 150 people. That is extreme, but it meant hundreds of thousands of people read something better.
>
> o We are okay with employee churn (in fact, I encourage it if it helps us ship a superior product).
>
> Lastly, it should be **considered a failure to receive feedback on something that could have made a creator's life better *after* you shipped.**

SEEK SUPERLINEARITIES

This value is a way to define and to encourage growth. Though superlinearity is a mathematical concept referring to a function that eventually grows faster than any linear one, at

Gumroad it represents our willingness to learn at a constantly accelerating pace.

How I communicate this internally:

> We have a fixed number of hours and an unlimited amount of creator income to actualize. Everything we do should contribute to our creators' bottom lines in a measurable and scalable way. **Every day you are producing superlinear returns on your time investment.**

What this means in practice is that job responsibilities at Gumroad change quickly. Employees might outgrow their roles and leave Gumroad to start their own companies. Great!

EVERYONE IS A CEO

This value is about building a company of like-minded people. I'm a CEO, and I think it's a pretty great job, so I want to create a company full of them.

How I communicate this internally:

> Ultimately, you are responsible for spending our creators' money, and it's your job to tell the company how you're doing that.
>
> You are the CEO of your function, and it is your responsibility to make sure it is executing at a high level and communicating proof to the rest of the company— and our creators.
>
> You need to think strategically (about business and product), proactively get things done, ask for help when needed, and hold yourself accountable before I need to.
>
> Similarly, don't waste resources:
>
> o Everyone is doing something important when you ask them for help, so do what you can to **save them**

time and expensive back-and-forth. This means providing all the context anyone needs, including objective measurements.

    o Think like a CEO asking for approval from their board, not like an employee asking their manager for direction. **If someone needs to ask you how things are going, they are not going well.**

Most people don't want to be CEOs; most people don't want to work for a company that has these expectations for its workforce. That's fine too; the people who do want to become CEOs find our situation appealing, and they're the ones I believe will create the most value for our creators anyway.

DARE TO BE OPEN

Given you're reading our internal values, this is likely the clearest of the bunch.

How I communicate this internally:

> If there's a Gumroad secret, it's this one: we aim for complete information symmetry. There's nothing I know that you don't, and eventually there'll be nothing you and I know that our creators don't.
>
> We are building the best product, with the best team, for the best community. Being open about everything is the flywheel that brings more amazing people into our ecosystem.

This manifests in numerous ways, like making our on-boarding documents publicly available and sharing our financials on Twitter every month. That way, not only does everyone who works at Gumroad know what we're about, but our customers and anyone who might even think about working at Gumroad knows too.

I recommend this level of transparency to everyone. The upside is that some of the people who get to know more about your company will love you. The downside is that some won't. They won't agree with the way you do business. They'll disagree with your policies on product quality and remote work or pick apart your numbers. Having a point of view and putting it into practice can be polarizing, but if what you're doing works for you, your customers, and your employees, and the company is profitable, you can sleep at night knowing you're doing the right thing. No one can take it away from you.

Another plus is that when things aren't going well, transparency can lead to the kind of reflection that will make things better. The most profound thing I have learned running a company has been the difference between behavior and intention. Behavior is what someone is doing; intention is why they're doing it. Most people judge themselves based on their own intentions but then judge others based on their behavior. Transparency makes that difficult, if not impossible.

As the CEO of an impactful company, it's important for me to be open about my intentions. Then others can look at my behavior and suggest improvements so that they match up better. Sunlight may not *always* be the best disinfectant, but it often helps.

Transparency isn't just about what we show to the world; it's also about how we operate internally. In chapter 3, I talked about the processes we use to run our business, all of which are documented and available for every employee to see. Day-to-day, we use tools such as Slack and Notion to keep every-one in our company aware of what is happening and to give employees clarity about how their work matters. It's easy for people to peer into anything if they're curious (or take over if need be). The cumulative effect of the open environment we've created with public numbers, no meetings, and open communication is that there are no secrets and no FOMO.

For example, everyone at Gumroad can see via an online dashboard how much our creators are earning. It does run the risk of creating a counterproductive obsession with the numbers (sometimes it is the founder's job to worry about the bottom line, not the employees'), but generally I've found that empowering your team with the data they need to make their own decisions creates a better, more self-sufficient organization. Plus, it means you need to do less, which is a big reason you chose to be a minimalist entrepreneur in the first place.

We also give everyone access to the traffic dashboards, and several of our engineers, when they are looking to take a break from their normal workload, will go in there and see what pages of the site they can speed up. These are things I may never have prioritized, but they save our customers time and improve our product offering.

Ultimately, if you hire well, your employees will be better managers of themselves than you could ever be. And in the long run, giving everyone autonomy allows you to be a peer to your employees so that you can code alongside your engi-neers, design alongside your designers, and spend your time creating and building something impactful rather than con-stantly managing others. As long as you continue to lay out the long-term vision for the company based on clearly artic-ulated values, your employees will be happy to support you.

Transparency also matters when it comes to the harder things like money. At Gumroad, we disclose everyone's salary in the company to everyone else, using a simple spreadsheet I keep up to date. This lets people feel good about how much they make and minimizes information asymmetry between me and the rest of the team. Revealing that kind of information may seem scary at first, but that's just because it's unusual. In practice it vastly reduces the number of questions people ask about their compensation, and it also helps combat wage disparity because of bias.

Laying out the numbers behind the business and the salaries you're paying people tells your employees how their work contributes to the overall profitability of the business. That information makes it easier for everyone when it comes time to have an honest conversation about how much they deserve to get paid. Global studies reveal that 79 percent of people who quit their jobs cite "lack of appreciation" as their reason for leaving, and though it's normal, even expected, for employees to outgrow your company and move on, you don't want unnecessary turnover to be a part of the culture of your business.

Beware of the Peter Principle

I don't like to manage. I would much rather have ten amazing people on my team than a hundred good ones. That might mean that we cannot ship as much code as the next startup on an absolute basis, but on a per-person basis we are far more productive and more fulfilled because of it.

Ultimately, a company scales successfully because employees are empowered to help customers without your intervention. Your job, and the job of any management team you build, is to give them the resources to succeed, and, when necessary, the thirty-thousand-foot view so they can clearly see where their work fits into the big picture without having to undertake the stressful process of investigating on their own.

Don't be a product visionary—or, worse, a product dictator. Your company shouldn't be a cult of personality, building exclusively what you want on the timelines you decide. WeWork is one example of how that path leads to certain doom. Among the numerous excesses, questionable decision making, and lavish capital infusions based on little evidence that the company might ever be profitable, one fascinating detail stands out. Even though WeWork's business has nothing to do with surfing, the board approved a $13 million investment in a company that made artificial wave pools because former CEO Adam Neumann is an avid surfer.

That, of course, is an extreme case of the ways in which a CEO's ideas and preferences, however irrational and counter to the interests of the business, can sink the business itself, but the point still stands. Whether you have three employees or three hundred, have clear key performance indicators (KPI) that *everyone* knows about and can measure their work against, which will allow *everyone* to either talk to or build for customers.

The Peter Principle, coined by educator Laurence J. Peter, states that "the tendency in most organization hierarchies, such as that of a corporation, is for every employee to rise in the hierarchy through promotion until they reach a level of respective incompetence."

Though it was originally meant as satire, you may be able to relate to the idea that within a strict hierarchy, everyone gets stuck with the job they're not good at. At Gumroad, I've tried to turn the Peter Principle on its head. Employees work for customers. I work for my employees. The best people continue to do the jobs they're best at as they get promoted—they just get paid more to do it.

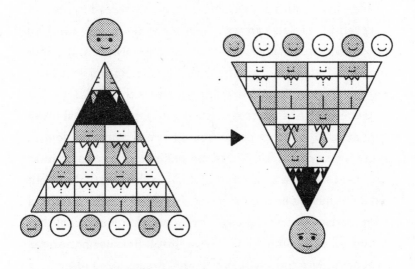

The problem with managers is that they aren't really invested in the success of the people they manage. But sometimes it's more than just being invested in your employees' success on the job; it's about caring about and investing in your employees' career aspirations and growth—beyond what your company might require. It's about the long-term game for everyone involved.

This might even mean encouraging your employees to leave to find more growth elsewhere, which we'll cover at the end of this chapter.

Create Accountability

Gumroad has been remote since 2015.

I think that remote work is going to be the norm for pretty much every business that doesn't need an office. Which is almost every business that pivoted and figured out a way to keep going with a distributed team during the COVID-19 pandemic.

When you don't have an office, you don't need to restrict yourself to the folks in your local geography. You can hire people across the world—finding the best people and bringing them into your company without either of you ever leaving home or needing to fly halfway across the world.

Once you've taken that step, you might realize that other conventional wisdom about how to run a company doesn't make sense either. Meetings, for example. Most companies use meetings as an essential tool to get their work done, but we don't have meetings at Gumroad. We've even taken it a step further: we're fully asynchronous. This has meant that for us, all communication is thoughtful. Because nothing is urgent—unless the site is down—discussion takes place only after mindful processing.

But what happens when something urgent *does* happen? The truth is that our business model doesn't produce the kind of "drop everything and deal with it now" situations that might occur if, for example, your company is reliant on business development and a key customer is pulling out because of a feature degradation or a missed deadline.

If something does require near-immediate engagement, we use Slack as our closest-to-real-time communication channel. GitHub is where we keep our codebase and where engineers submit their code for peer review before it is merged in and deployed live. Notion is for everything else. It is what we use to host our roadmap (which we make public) and our product development processes, as well as where we house our knowledge sharing around how each person does their job.

This three-pronged system is a useful heuristic to help employees know where to go to get help when they need it. In a few hours, Slack. In a day or two, GitHub. Longer than that, Notion. Transparency around metrics and team compensation is important—but it's also important to make it easy to surface the right information at the right time for the right people.

If something does need to be discussed in really-real time, we now use Clubhouse for audio-only conversations. As a bonus, we can pull our customers into meetings much more easily than if it were a Zoom call.

This culture requires everyone to tell everyone else when they plan to do "deep work," a term coined by writer Cal Newport indicating focused, cognitively demanding tasks. Much of the work we do, including writing, coding, and designing, doesn't lend itself well to interruptions. Beyond setting expectations, people can decide how they wish to implement this. They can let others know when they plan to surface and respond to questions, or they can turn off their notifications for weeks on end. For me, this is as simple as blocking out times in my calendar.

Clear expectations around availability allow people to build their work around their life, not the other way around. This is especially great for new parents, but everyone benefits from being able to structure their days to maximize their happiness and productivity, and most people can learn to manage themselves and be productive and impactful.

I recognize that what I do and what we do at Gumroad may not work for every founder or every company, depending on the nature of the business. While flexible work hours are becoming more common, some companies function best when they are totally asynchronous and remote like us, while others use a hybrid of remote work and shared time at coworking spaces. As long as you keep a laser focus on delivering the best product to your customers, creating a system that works will develop organically from the bottom up rather than feeling like something dictated from the top.

Ultimately, it's up to you to decide what kind of house you want to live in and then find people who agree. Gumroad's values are a little offbeat. You might even say they're a little scary. But they guide everything we do, and they communicate what the world needs to know about our company. Our values may not work for most people. For them, Gumroad isn't a fit. Luckily, there are millions of other companies that are.

How Simply Eloped Defined Its Values and Got Back on Track

Hiring before defining your values and culture is a challenge many founders face, perhaps because it is the default, but luckily it's an issue you can come back from.

Janessa White and Matt Dalley are two founders who ran into trouble when they started hiring at Simply Eloped, a company that helps couples plan intimate or destination weddings. Up until then, Matt and Janessa had been doing everything right. They grew slowly and were strategic about every dollar they spent. Before they started hiring, they had performed every function—customer service, marketing, sales—themselves, and it had allowed them to develop their own systems and to be adaptable and creative, especially when it came to money.

They had also made conscious choices about the vendors they hired to represent Simply Eloped. "The wedding industry can be full of discrimination, so from the very beginning, we built relationships with officiants, florists, bakers, and others who shared our values and felt comfortable with all sorts of couples. I had spent years talking with customers," Janessa said, "and I knew that we were offering the kind of affordable, inclusive service that people couldn't find anywhere else."

Even though Matt and Janessa had been deliberate about the kinds of external relationships they wanted to cultivate, they hadn't been as intentional about the culture they wanted to build inside Simply Eloped. In 2019, they raised capital and began a hiring push. "We made every mistake in the book," they said. "We hired for our wish list, we hired friends and family, and we hired anyone who seemed nice and wanted a job." The result was what Janessa called a "cultural crisis" during which bullying, gossip, and drama became commonplace.

Their first step to correcting course was to hire a leadership coach who began the process of identifying what was happening and how to fix it. Matt and Janessa were forced to ask themselves what kind of leaders they needed to be to manage a growing team. They saw that they had focused too much on making their employees "happy" and not enough time defining what would best serve their customers and provide the best work atmosphere.

They also realized that even though *they* and many of their customers loved the company, it wasn't going to be the right fit for everyone. This revelation sent them back to the drawing board to consider their values, which they now define using the acronym CACAO, for "customer-centric, ambitious, compassionate, adaptable, and ownership." What's more, they translated those values into a list of attributes that describe the type of person who will thrive at Simply Eloped, and they now draw from that list for their job postings.

In addition, Janessa, Matt, and their team explicitly use Simply Eloped's values to highlight success and to give feedback; during the weekly announcements, Janessa weaves in company values to tell stories about employees' small wins; on the flip side, if someone isn't performing well, she can use the values as context for how and why to improve. Values have ended up being so important at Simply Eloped that Matt and Janessa even wrote a song about them that every employee learns.

While you may not want or need to write a song about your company values (we definitely are never going to write a song at Gumroad), it's worth noting how clearly Janessa and Matt articulate and define the company's values, for themselves and for everyone who works there. They've found something that works for them, and their clear values enable them to grow knowing where they're going and who they want to bring along with them.

Tell the World Who You Are

Ultimately, it will be more work to build your company culture than your product. But it will also be more valuable. And at the end of it, you will have a company that fulfills your goals and the goals of many others as well.

People do not change jobs often, and they often don't declare to the world when they're thinking about doing so. In chapter 5, we talked about how marketing is about reminding prospective customers that you exist, over and over again. Similarly, hiring well is about reminding prospective candidates that you exist, and why you exist, over and over again.

And just like we learned in chapter 4, good sales isn't just about sales—it's about education. Hiring is one of the hardest things about startups, because it's about product development, sales, and marketing—all at once!

Once you have cultural values that work for you, start to communicate them publicly. Many people fear that communicating these values will alienate people from looking further into their company. This is exactly correct. Clearly defining your cultural values allows most folks to say, "This isn't for me," and a select few to say, "THIS IS EXACTLY THE JOB FOR ME!"

Great people will only apply if they see a job that matches (or exceeds) their expectations for what their ideal work life could be like. If you can, reflect on any painful or stressful job searches you've had, and how often you've gotten to the end of a long interview process with a company only to realize they weren't a fit for you *at all*.

Communicating your values saves everyone time and energy. You only want to interview the candidates who think they're a really good fit for you, not people who are just looking for their next job or a pay raise. Ultimately, the greatest candidates are the ones who plan to replace you.

Hiring Looks a Lot Like Firing Yourself

From the beginning, you should look to hire people who are better than you. They're not there to implement your vision but to improve upon it based on their own interactions with customers.

Some of them may even be your previous customers. At Gumroad, we make a point to hire from our community first.

Many founders fail to delegate well, but it begins with self-awareness. Ask yourself:

o What do I most enjoy doing?
o What am I good at, and what am I not so good at?
o What function would be a relief to pass to someone else?
o How do I spend most of my time, and is that the right choice?

Once you figure out exactly what job you are hiring for, you can figure out who may be a fit. But often you won't know. Again, this is why it's important to get good at shouting into the ether and letting people come to you.

Your job listings should be a filter, not a magnet. Most people won't enjoy working at your company, and your job listings should make it clear that they should look elsewhere. The people who get all the way through are the ones you should have more serious conversations with.

If you do this well, hiring becomes much easier and faster. And because of your minimalist approach to building your business, you already have communities, customers, and a marketing muscle with which to best engage them.

For example, a single tweet from my personal Twitter account led to hundreds of applicants:

Sahil ✔ @shl · Aug 6, 2020
We're looking for engineers who want to work on @gumroad!

- Web (Ruby + JS) or iOS (Swift)
- 20+ hours a week
- $125-$200/hr
- Work from anywhere, no scheduled meetings, no deadlines
- Everything you work on will eventually be OSS!

💬 75   🔁 361   ♡ 1.2K   ⬆️

This isn't just true for me. Adam Wathan's single tweet about a job working on Tailwind UI led to 875 applicants. His tweet, similar to mine, was clear and opinionated:

Adam Wathan   •••
@adamwathan

If you're interested in building UI tools with me full-time, we're looking for a developer to join the Tailwind CSS team.

$115k–$135k/year, 4 weeks vacation, and 40 hours a week of hacking on fun, interesting problems.

1:32 PM · May 24, 2020 · Twitter for iPhone

598 Retweets   **56** Quote Tweets   **1,833** Likes

Revisit your values, and make sure they are embedded in your job post just like everything else that you write. For Gumroad that means making it clear how much we pay, what we expect of our people, and what we don't offer. But your values will be different from ours, and so your job posts will be too.

Fit Is Two-Way

Unfortunately, not everyone who joins your company will stick around for the long term, or maybe even the short term. Fit is two-way; when someone isn't working out for you, it also means you aren't working out for them. And someone who isn't a great fit for your company is hurting their own long-term prospects just like they are hurting yours.

When in doubt, reflect on your values. Does this person match? Would this person be *creating more value* outside of your company than within it? Would you hire them today if you knew then what you know now?

Truthfully, when you start doubting, you probably know the answer and just aren't comfortable making the hard decision of letting them go.

Believe me, I know how difficult it is to fire people. But it is an essential skill if you want to build the house you want to live in. To my people, I promise no surprises. Even if it's not a fit, I make it clear—and, due to our asynchronous culture, in writing—exactly why I have concerns that it may not be a fit, corresponding each issue with our values. I do this at least twice over several weeks, making sure they have the clarity and time to make the changes I need them to make.

But ultimately it's their choice, and often the best thing you can do is to have an honest conversation, tell them it's not working out, and wind things down. Almost every time, they'll be grateful you brought it up instead of them. And if you've been hiring well, they'll find a new job in no time at all. And you should help them with that, providing introductions and a positive reference—you did hire them, after all. They weren't bad employees, they just weren't a fit for you.

Your company is a business, not a cult. Embrace change, don't abhor it.

Speaking of change. . . . At this point you'll have a product that customers are happy paying for and a company that people are happy to work for. What comes next?

If you're having fun, you can keep doing what you're doing. Or you can do something completely new. That's what the next chapter is about. We'll talk about broadening and deepening your impact, as well as how to improve your own quality of life. On some level, that's what this whole book has been about: identifying and helping those you love—including yourself—in a way that aligns your own life with the lives of others. Let's go.

KEY TAKEAWAYS

o You've already built one product for customers, now you're building another: The product is your company, and your customers are your employees.

o Building a company full of humans is more rewarding than building software, but it is also much harder.

o Articulate your values early and often, because you will need them to avoid veering off course as you grow. (It'll happen anyway.)

o Fit is two-way: If it's not working out for you, it's probably not working out for them. Have the hard conversations early, as they'll only get harder the longer you wait.

Learn More

- o Read *Reinventing Organizations,* a book by Frédéric Laloux, for a mind-bending look into how the structures of companies and other organizations have changed over time.
- o Follow Janessa White, co-CEO and cofounder of Simply Eloped, on Twitter (@janessanwhite) for insights from building her business.
- o Read *The Peter Principle,* a book by Laurence J. Peter and Raymond Hull.

8

where do we go from here?

We are born to wander through a chaos field.
And yet we do not become hopelessly lost,
because each walker who comes before us leaves
behind a trace for us to follow.

—ROBERT MOOR

This chapter comes last, but I rank it first in significance.

Even after reading this book, you may be asking yourself if now is the best time to start a company. There is a lot broken with the world, and the future is uncertain. If you think starting a business looks risky, you're right: It is and always will be. But I believe it's one of the best ways to make change.

Never mind if your business isn't "changing the world" from day one, or doesn't employ hundreds of people. As long as you're making the world better in an honest, scalable way by selling a product worth paying for to a community that wants it, starting a company is worth it.

I don't think healing the world only happens if we are able to make "a dent in the universe," as Steve Jobs is famously misquoted; it also comes about by repeatedly making small choices that compound and that improve our communities. You can't change everything, but you can and should change a few things, to start.

The reward, once you're profitable and growing sustainably because your customers are spreading the word, is that you get to decide what your company's next positive impact will be. I know that once Gumroad got to that point, it was easier for me to focus on a more meaningful life. But it still wasn't easy. I had to wrestle with a new definition of success, one that would be defined by a greater sense of purpose and mission.

"A healthy man wants a thousand things, a sick man only wants one," Confucius is purported to have said. Rephrased in the context of this book, a minimalist entrepreneur without a successful, sustainable business only wants one thing (that!), while one who has achieved it has the world as their

oyster. And Søren Kierkegaard wrote in 1844 that anxiety is the "dizziness of freedom." It's what happens when you stare at the infinity of your own choices.

This is all part of what you get—for taking the risk, doing the hard work, and putting in the time to start and to scale your business—whether you like it or not. Now that you've arrived at your initial destination, *where do you go next?* That's what we'll spend this last chapter trying to answer.

You've Made Money, Now Make Time

The first thing I did when Gumroad became profitable was to reclaim a significant part of my time.

I had lived the founder life for four years, working whenever I wasn't sleeping, neglecting relationships with friends and family, and generally putting work ahead of all else. With all that behind me, I was free to chart a different course. I found that when I wasn't trying to placate investors or make the company grow faster than it was meant to grow, finally, I had time. While I was no longer on track to become a dollar billionaire, I realized I was a "time billionaire," someone Graham Duncan defines as having at least a billion seconds left in their life—or at least thirty-one years.

I didn't have a billion bucks, but I did have the luxury (or agony, depending on how you see it) of obligation-free days for the first time in a long time. I rented a modest apartment in Provo, gave up coffee and beer, and started meeting people who shared my creative interests. After years during which work was the crux of my identity, I wanted the rest of my life to be about anything else.

First off: using my time to create more time. I accomplished that by further automating, outsourcing, or outright ignoring everything related to Gumroad I didn't enjoy doing (see chapters 3 and 6). That way, I had as much time to do whatever I wanted, whenever I wanted to do it. Is this possible for everyone and every business? I'm not certain. But I do think that you'd be surprised at all the stuff you don't need to do if you extricate yourself from situations and obligations your former self would have considered essential.

Then I went back to the beginning of my journey: I started creating again. First, I wrote fantasy in Provo as part of a creative writing workshop taught by Brandon Sanderson, one of my favorite authors. Afterward, I stuck around Utah and learned to paint. It probably isn't a surprise, given that I run a company that employs and serves creators, but I like creating stuff.

Creating ex nihilo is satisfying and fun, especially when it doesn't need to pay the bills, and running a minimalist business allowed me to progress at a rapid pace. At some points, I spent upwards of twenty hours a week writing and painting. (And I haven't stopped!)

But for me, making stuff doesn't complete me, just like chasing unicorns didn't. I still cared about having a large impact on the world, and I still had a business to help me do it. I didn't need Gumroad to be a billion-dollar company to be free to pursue my goals with maximal optionality and minimal baggage. And I promise that you don't need your business to be that big, either, to accomplish all you hope to accomplish.

I believe our goal should be to bring together our passions, our missions, our professions, and our vocations. This is the Japanese concept of *ikigai*, which aligns what you love, with what the world needs, with what you can be paid for, and with what you are good at:

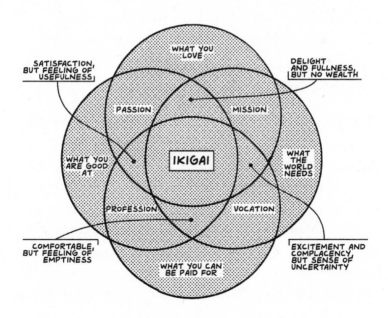

When you are in *ikigai*, you feel at peace, and you can work to improve the world at the same time. You can live in the present while working toward a better future.

I believe strongly that the arc of humanity is in its infancy, and one of the major ways we'll continue to make progress is via mindful business creation. One key reason I've used the word "minimalist" to describe entrepreneurship in this book is because I believe your business does not need to be the answer to every question. Becoming a minimalist entrepreneur may result in a great outcome for you while also creating opportunities for your team and your community, but it is unlikely to solve every problem you encounter, either for yourself or for the world.

The goal here is to *free* yourself, to make the business require as little of you as you wish it to, so that you can engage with the world in the way you think best, whatever that looks like. For most, that means *freeing* others too. You can't free everyone, or build every business, but you can at least teach a few people how.

Create More Creators, CEOs, and Minimalist Entrepreneurs

After two years in Provo, I had a new perspective on Gumroad and my mission. When I reimagined the future, I realized I had the chance not only to make a life for myself but also to expand opportunities for others to make a life for themselves.

Building Gumroad exposed me to a whole new range of creators: business owners. Not every act of creation requires a business, but many creators who reach scale start a business to manage their work. One of the things I'm proudest of is that

I've made the business side of creation easier for thousands of other people and created business owners around the world.

In 2020, I stumbled upon the next step in my journey to make entrepreneurship accessible to all. Up until then, I had experimented in investing in early-stage tech startups by becoming a limited partner in Arlan Hamilton's Backstage Capital and making several small angel investments in start-ups such as Lambda School, Figma, and Notion. But in the wake of the George Floyd protests in 2020, I knew I could do more, and I tweeted about wanting to invest in Black founders:

 Sahil ✔
@shl

Occasionally I angel invest in tech startups, including @LambdaSchool, @figmadesign, @HelloSign. I'm also an LP in @Backstage_Cap.

My next investment will be in a Black founder. If you are one, please send me an email this week about what you're working on: sahil@hey.com

9:00 AM · Jun 1, 2020 · Twitter Web App

237 Retweets **30** Quote Tweets **1,306** Likes

That tweet led to two hundred emails from Black founders and—most important—four new investments in startups founded by Black entrepreneurs. Since then, there have been several more through in-network referrals.

But many of these startups were looking to raise more capital, and I didn't have very much. So I wrote a "memo" and emailed other investors in my network. One responded, "You should start a fund," and offered to anchor it to help get it off the ground. I doubled down on my goal of creating more CEOs and minimalist entrepreneurs and launched my own fund last year.

Even though I never expected to be a venture capitalist myself, I am now able to support the kind of founders I meet primarily through my audience and through building Gumroad openly and transparently. Today I get to invest approximately $10 million a year in about fifty companies.

I still turn many founders away, but that's not necessarily because I don't believe in what they're doing. It's because most businesses would be better off without venture capital. Ever since I published "Reflecting on My Failure to Build a Billion-Dollar Company" in February 2019, I've met hundreds of minimalist entrepreneurs who have helped me widen my mental model for what a business really is.

If you think becoming a minimalist entrepreneur was a good thing for you, you can help other people see the way. Peter Askew regularly tweets out domain names that he thinks would make great businesses so that others can follow in his footsteps. Chris Cantino and Jaime Schmidt of Schmidt's Naturals started their own investment fund, Color, which supports and invests in underrepresented founders.

Being a creator and a minimalist entrepreneur is a path that should be available to a huge array of different kinds of people, and all different kinds of employees and customers should be able to find the exact right fit for themselves. I would argue that it should be available to all eight billion people on this planet. Alas, we're not there yet.

Though minimalist businesses cannot eliminate discrimination or repair every disparity in access to education, technology, and funding, they do offer a pathway for a wide variety of entrepreneurs to take control of their own destinies.

Furthermore, I believe the path to a more equitable future is for more people to create a product or service and sell that, not only because it allows business owners to make a living from creating but also because by expanding the reach of entrepreneurship we can serve people whose problems have not yet been addressed by the free market.

Ultimately, it's up to everyone to decide how they want to run their life and their business. Moving from San Francisco to Provo reminded me that people have their own visions of how they want to serve others. It's not one-size-fits-all, not even close, nor should it be. Different people have different problems and require different solutions.

SAN FRANCISCO

PROVO

Save the Planet

We've talked about the myth of "changing the world" being a distraction from the forest of great business and community-serving opportunities you're already in.

But you can still pick battles to fight, especially things that are within your control, like offsetting your carbon footprint and committing to a carbon-neutral future. Large organizations, which fuel the systems and servers that many minimalist entrepreneurs use to power their businesses, are accelerating this process and making it more straightforward to commit to carbon neutrality. In 2019, Shopify committed at least $5 million annually to the Shopify Sustainability Fund, which will invest not only in carbon sequestration but also in renewable energy and more sustainable operations for both merchants and buyers. By 2030, Google has committed to running on carbon-free energy everywhere at all times.

But it's not just about relying on big business and its infrastructure to do the work. We can use our companies to make our own contributions to saving the planet no matter what size they are. Emily LaFave Olson, founder of Rainbow Road, a plant-based ice-cream company, is committed to using food as a tool to heal the planet. After she sold her first company, Foodzie, an online gourmet marketplace, and closed her second, Din, a meal kit delivery service, she too found herself asking, "What's next?"

Her personal mission was to get closer to the earth, and she and her family moved to Hawaii as she considered her next venture. One idea kept coming to mind: ice cream.

She set out to build Rainbow Road into a company that makes delicious ice cream by way of a full-cycle, circular system that is good for the earth. "*Pono* is a word in Hawaiian that means harmonious," she says, "and I keep the company and myself in balance by always keeping our mission in mind as I make decisions and tell our story."

Having raised venture capital for her two previous companies, she's committed to bootstrapping for now in order to preserve full decision-making control and to focus on profitability and taking her time. "I'm creating longevity by building a foundation more slowly," she says, "so I ask my-self, 'What is the next smallest step I can take?'" That has allowed Rainbow Road to grow in a way that feels sustainable for the company and for the world. "I can grow something really substantial with baby steps, so I'm not afraid of taking the longer path."

Do your research, figure out what really works, and start putting your mouth where your money is.

Let Go

I haven't taken this path yet, but I've thought about it. One day I may want even *more* of my time back, or I may want to serve a totally different group of people in a totally different way. Just like I don't expect anyone else to work at Gumroad forever, I don't expect to either. Ultimately, I will let it go, either by choice or by force—and I certainly hope it's the former.

You will ultimately have to make the same kind of decisions. You may walk away from your business completely. You may retire on a beach and feel like your work is done. You may decide to double down, raise money, and take a big swing with your next company. You may find a new CEO but stay involved in the running of the company as chairperson of the board, or start a nonprofit to tackle the next problem you find.

But where *specifically* do you go from here?

The answer is that I don't know. This question never goes away, and there will never be one right answer for every founder. This is why you should always try to build the right business for yourself *selfishly* while at the same time also serving a community of others *selflessly*. And you should prioritize your happiness while you do it!

I know it's a lot to ask, but it's time to ask yourself *why*.

You picked a community. *Why* that one? You shipped a manual valuable process and then iterated it into a minimum viable product. *Why* did you choose to solve those problems in the ways that you did?

If memory serves, you then sold that product to a hundred customers, who happily paid for it. Who did you reach out to first, and *why* them?

You marketed the business and grew yourself and your team alongside it. *Why, why, why?*

And finally: *Why* do I want to move on from here? *Why* do I need to go anywhere at all?

What helped me, and what will help you as you tackle these questions, is to spend your newfound time reflecting on your past and observing your present to figure out who you are and what you really want. Then you can figure out how to get what you want so you can stop asking these questions at all.

Your "purpose" may be to create more creators, or to help more people start businesses, or to retire on a beach and spend all your time surfing. I won't pretend to know.

My goal in this book was to give you the tools that would enable you to build a business that ultimately gives you the choice and freedom to decide for yourself. It's up to you now. *What's next?*

Whatever you do, send me a message and let me know. I'm on the internet:

sahil@hey.com

one more thing

Let's start at the beginning. What's the plan? You have a business idea, hopefully. And because you picked the right community to serve, and became a pillar within it, you have a good plan of attack to get started on building your MVP (manual valuable process first, then a minimum viable product). You're going to get to a hundred customers, and only *then* worry about launching!

Soon after—or maybe you're already there—you will be profitable and in control of your destiny. You'll learn how to stay there as you get a good grip on the legal, operational, and financial components of running your business.

You'll craft a culture that attracts the kind of people you love working with and for. It won't be easy, but your business will grow, and you will start to solve new problems over time.

Most important, your identity will not be wrapped up in your business. You won't need to do anything you don't want to, at least not for more than a couple of hours a week. Take that, Tim!

Of course, even then the journey isn't over. It never is. It won't be easy or quick or straightforward. It will take a lot of time, and perhaps a few attempts, but that's okay, because you have a whole life ahead of you to figure things out. And it's not about avoiding failure but getting to success, eventually. The longer it takes to win, the more prepared you'll be, because you will get better every year that it takes.

In this book, we've mostly spoken about successful businesses. But every successful entrepreneur has many failed attempts. In the years before Gumroad's creation, I built and launched several dozen things. Almost all of them failed. Gumroad worked, though. And you only need to be right once.

But humanity needs millions if we hope to get out of this mess. (We'll always be in a mess.) Regardless, I believe the future of entrepreneurship *is* the future of humanity, and so the more companies that get started the better. And the best way to get more companies started is to make it easy, accessible, and attainable.

I'm not trying to convince you. Rather, I think you'll understand it deeply when you're running your own business. Your work is necessary. The business you will start is necessary. These kinds of businesses have been necessary for hundreds of years and will be for thousands of years more. There's nothing new about them.

If you're struggling to even come up with a problem to solve, be patient. Look around and pay attention. Humanity is just getting started, and it's unlikely that *anything* we do today will resemble how we do it in the future.

One day, your life and work will align. You'll have a purpose that unifies everything you do. You'll get paid to do what you love. Your business will grow as long as you keep being *you*.

All of these things will happen. But only if you do the most important thing and . . .

Start.

ACKNOWLEDGMENTS

Family first: my mom, Shamina Lavingia, and my dad, Ayaz Lavingia, and my brother, Samir Lavingia, for creating and shaping me. And my wife, Kaede Takeshige, for bearing with and encouraging me all the while.

Like all the businesses mentioned in this book, *The Minimalist Entrepreneur* is the product of a community.

The idea originally came from Merry Sun, my editor at Penguin Random House. She read my viral Medium post and suggested that we talk if I was at all interested in "expanding [the] Medium post into a nonfiction book." That was in February 2019.

Merry introduced me to Lisa DiMona, who became my literary agent at Writer's House. Together, they encouraged me to move beyond my initial favorite title, *Leaving Startupland,* and helped me zero in on the topic of this book—businesses that focus on "creating value" in a sustainable way. They also made me realize I wasn't going to be able to do it myself.

David Moldawer helped me take my initial outline and transform it into something that had real structure. He also came up with a much better title: *Stop Chasing Unicorns*. I felt really great about the whole thing and signed a book deal with Penguin. That was in December 2019.

I started writing in earnest in January 2020. Then COVID happened. Gumroad started to grow like a weed, and I—along with the rest of the world—had an identity crisis. On the one hand, Gumroad was suddenly on its way (again) to becoming a "unicorn," but on the other, I was not interested in getting back on the VC hamster wheel. I wanted to craft a third way for myself, and in some ways already had; the way I ran Gumroad—fully remote and with no meetings since 2016— meant I was more prepared for the pandemic than many of my peers.

I was also a lot busier. I completed the first draft of the book by summer 2020, but it wasn't good enough. It was too negative (*Stop Chasing Unicorns* doesn't tell you what you *should* do), and it wasn't backed up with enough anecdotes and real data. And frankly, representation was a problem.

Lisa suggested I work with Julie Mosow to help me take the book "over the finish line." Together, Julie and I finished the second draft of the book in December 2020. We changed the name to *The Minimalist Startup*, and then *The Minimalist Entrepreneur*. Almost two years into writing the book, I finally understood what this book was meant to be about all along. It's about a new kind of human and a new kind of lifestyle that software has enabled through "permissionless leverage." The year 2020 gave the world a peek into the future, and I happened to already be living in it. Another example why you should start, then learn.

Together, Merry, Lisa, David, Julie, and I are responsible for most of the words in the book. But the writing process didn't end there! In February 2020, I taught a cohort-based course to test the ideas in the book and make sure they resonated. Each week, the 136 "students" read and gave feedback chapter by chapter. At the end of the month, we had hundreds of comments—about what was boring, confusing, or implausible—to address.

Those students—and coaches—include: Bhaumik, Timothy, Jonah, Shane, Somvir, Shahena, Jens, Nasir, Robin, Akash, Jamil, Dario, Covington, Adam, Kirill, Ganesh, James, Carlos, Karl, Asim, Surya, Binh, Josh, Rajat, Aneesh, Ditri, Karan, Yousef, Yousef-Husaini, Rahul, Dhruba, Hera, Brian, Addy, Padi, Michael, Matthew, Andrew, Preetham, Matthew, Marty, Vaughan, Shaik, Manuel, Ari, Prab, Isaac, Jon, Nick, Mukesh, Julian, Chandan, Gagan, Rachel, Sergio, Sahil, Shawn, Monte, Aman, Theola, Amin, Pradeep, Prolok, Sam, Greg, Woody, Evan, Sean, Ashray, Eli, Manan, Ozgur, Scott, Shirish, Gerben, Justin, Ciprian, Ahmed, Ashwin, Josh, Obaid, Carl, Nara, Sridhar, Andrew, Alex, Clint, Nick, Mike, Marvin, Bugi, Amar, Wes, Lia, Crystal, Michael, Mert, Tribe, Workast, Yasaman, Manish, David, Raphael, Mateo, Nate, Tobin, Mike, Hunter, Michael, Sergey, Aravind, Akhil, Yazane, Sergio, John, Riddhi, Yuhan, Simon, Daniel, Luca, Carlos, Razvan, Lorenzo, Eduardo, Murat, Devan, Ben, Marcos, Assim, Francis, Vishal, Thomas, Raul, Vladimir, Prashanth, Ralph, Pramod, Inga, Soumya, Louise, Zach, Nate, Soleil, Clark, Sagar, Charles, Albert, Connor, Gonzalo, Marissa, Clement, Nate, Minjun, Vince, Monish, Amaan, Joshua, Justin, Jenny, and Audrey.

And address we did. So if you liked the book, it's due to a *community* of just about 150 people. And if you didn't like the book . . . Well, it was all me!

Dillon Blue and Amy Stellhorn from Big Monocle designed the cover with help from Brian Lemus and Jen Heuer from Penguin Random House. The illustrations are by Brian Box Brown.

I'd also like to thank the rest of the folks at Penguin who worked on and championed the book behind the scenes, including Adrian Zackheim, Tara Gilbride, Niki Papadopoulos, Jessica Regione, Gabriel Levinson, Regina Andreoni, and Olivia Decker.

And thank *you* for reading!

NOTES

INTRODUCTION

vii   **"Just had an idea for my first"**: Sahil Lavingia, Twitter post, April 2, 2011, 2:45 a.m., https://twitter.com/shl/status/54072049395712000.

CHAPTER 1. THE MINIMALIST ENTREPRENEUR

1   **"The beginnings of all things"**: Cicero, *De finibus bonorum et malorum*, book V, chapter 58.

4   **"the domain name"**: Peter Askew, "I Sell Onions on the Internet," Deep South Ventures, April 2019, https://deepsouthventures.com /i-sell-onions-on-the-internet/.

4   **In 2009, that domain name**: Peter Askew, "The Dude That Built DudeRanch.com," Deep South Ventures, September 2019, https:// deepsouthventures.com/dude-that-built-duderanch-com/.

4   **In 2014, Askew saw**: Askew, "I Sell Onions on the Internet."

5   **"[The domain] kept nudging me"**: Askew, "I Sell Onions on the Internet."

5 **"I'm not a farmer":** Askew, "I Sell Onions on the Internet."

6 **Askew and Haygood estimated:** Askew, "I Sell Onions on the Internet."

6 **he was having fun:** Askew, "I Sell Onions on the Internet."

7 **"Honestly, my customers":** Askew, "I Sell Onions on the Internet."

9 **"product-market fit":** Marc Andreessen, "The Pmarca Guide to Startups," Pmarchive, June 25, 2007, https://pmarchive.com/guide _to_startups_part4.html.

12 **more than $1 billion:** Aileen Lee, "Welcome to the Unicorn Club: Learning from Billion-Dollar Startups," *TechCrunch*, November 2, 2013, https://techcrunch.com/2013/11/02/welcome-to-the-unicorn -club/.

12 **According to Matt Murphy:** David Baeza, "70% of Startups Fail. How Not to Become a Statistic," *Medium*, February 13, 2018, https://me dium.com/@davidbaeza/70-of-startups-fail-how-not-to -become-a-statistic-f4820144a973.

12 **The whole system is:** Baeza, "70% of Startups Fail."

CHAPTER 2: START WITH COMMUNITY

24 **Sol and Kurtis saw:** Sol Orwell, interview with Eric Siu, *Leveling Up*, podcast audio, June 9, 2019, https://www.levelingup.com/growth -everywhere-interview/sol-orwell-examine-com/.

24 **In 2011, they launched:** Benji Hyam, "How Examine.com Founder Sol Orwell Built a 7-Figure Business off of Reddit," Grow and Convert, April 13, 2018, https://growandconvert.com/marketing/exam ine-sol-orwell-reddit/.

24 **"100,000 plus karma":** Orwell, *Leveling Up*.

24 **a measure of how much:** "What Is Karma?," Reddit Help, https:// reddit.zendesk.com/hc/en-us/articles/204511829-What-is-karma.

25 **guide to supplements and nutrition:** Hyam, "How Examine Founder Sol Orwell Built a 7-Figure Business off of Reddit."

25 **By the end of the launch:** Hyam, "How Examine Founder Sol Orwell Built a 7-Figure Business off of Reddit."

25 **day-to-day operations:** "About Sol Orwell and Why SJO.com," SJO .com, August 9, 2018, https://www.sjo.com/about.

29 **the "passion economy":** Li Jin, "The Passion Economy and the Future of Work," Andreessen Horowitz, October 8, 2019, https://a16z.com/2019/10/08/passion-economy/.

29 **"a world in which":** Atelier Ventures, https://www.atelierventures.co/.

29 **"turn their passions into livelihoods":** Jin, "The Passion Economy and the Future of Work."

33 **the "1% Rule":** Jackie Huba and Ben McConnell, *Citizen Marketers: When People Are the Message* (Chicago: Kaplan Publishing, 2007).

35 **"Work in Public":** Nathan Barry, Twitter post, March 26, 2016, 10:29 a.m., https://twitter.com/nathanbarry/status/713734553257390080.

36 **"I realized I would take":** Nathan Barry, "How Teaching Everything I Know Grew My Audience," ConvertKit, November 18, 2019, https://convertkit.com/teaching-everything-know-grew-audience.

37 **become a cult classic:** Patrick McKenzie, "Salary Negotiation: Make More Money, Be More Valued," Kalzumeus Software, n.d., https://www.kalzumeus.com/2012/01/23/salary-negotiation.

37 **He now works for Stripe:** Patrick McKenzie, "What Working at Stripe Has Been Like," Kalzumeus Software, October 9, 2020, https://kalzumeus.com/2020/10/09/four-years-at-stripe.

43 **In 2020, Calendly posted:** Lucinda Shen, "Meet the Unicorn Founder That Braved War Zones and Missed Meetings to Make His Mark on the Startup World," *Fortune*, November 24, 2020, https://fortune.com/2020/11/19/calendly-founder-tope-awotona-startup-unicorn.

43 **"I didn't know anything":** Karen Houghton, "Tope Awotona—A Founder Story," *Atlanta Tech Village* (blog), April 26, 2018, https://atlantatechvillage.com/buzz/2018/04/26/tope-awotona-a-founder-story.

44 **both solve *and* monetize:** Stephanie Heath, "The Founder of Calendly on Building a Unicorn Tech Company," Mogul Millennial, May 23, 2021, https://www.mogulmillennial.com/the-founder-of-calendly-shares/.

44 **"What [great companies]":** Clayton M. Christensen, Taddy Hall, Karen Dillon, and David S Duncan, "Know Your Customers' 'Jobs to Be Done,'" *Harvard Business Review*, September 2016.

44 **"Nearly half the milkshakes"**: Clayton M. Christensen, Keynote Address, Techpoint Innovation Summit, Indianapolis, September 29, 2009.

47 **One business that provides**: Michael Ortiz, "Interview with TheCut App CEO on Modernizing Barbershop Experience," *Modern Treatise*, March 28, 2018, https://www.moderntreatise.com/business /2018/3/27/an-interview-with-the-ceo-of-thecut-app.

49 **"We went looking"**: Jason Fried, "Basecamp: The Origin Story," *Medium*, October 7, 2015, https://medium.com/@jasonfried/base camp-the-origin-story-f509fdd725f8.

49 **"We decided early"**: Fried, "Basecamp: The Origin Story."

49 **In a bid to solve**: Erin DeJesus, "Introducing Nick Kokonas's Ticketing System, Tock," *Eater*, November 30, 2014, https://www.eater .com/2014/11/30/7294795/introducing-nick-kokonass -ticketing-system-tock.

50 **During the COVID-19 pandemic**: Christina Troitino, "Reservation Service Tock Launches To-Go Platform to Help Restaurants Impacted by Coronavirus," *Forbes*, March 17, 2020, https://www .forbes.com/sites/christinatroitino/2020/03/17/reservation -service-tock-launches-to-go-platform-to-help-restaurants -impacted-by-coronavirus/.

CHAPTER 3: BUILD AS LITTLE AS POSSIBLE

55 **"Make something people want"**: Geoff Ralston and Michael Seibel, "YC's Essential Startup Advice," YC Startup Library, n.d., https:// www.ycombinator.com/library/4D-yc-s-essential-startup-advice.

61 **"If you want to make"**: Derek Sivers, *Anything You Want: 40 Lessons for a New Kind of Entrepreneur* (New York: Portfolio/Penguin, 2011).

62 **"Creating a product"**: Naval Ravikant (navalr), "Creating a product is a process of discovery, not mere implementation. Technology is applied science. Would a scientist outsource the discovery process?," Reddit, https://www.reddit.com/r/NavalRavikant/comments /dzio7t/ask_naval_anything/.

63 **they set up a Google Sheet**: John Eremic, "Growing a SaaS App for the Film Industry with Rigorous Experimentation," Indie Hackers,

n.d., https://www.indiehackers.com/interview/growing-a-saas-app
-for-the-film-industry-with-rigorous-experimentation-8aa8348dae.

63 **Their initial process:** Eremic, "Growing a SaaS App for the Film Industry."

64 **Forms of self-employment income for developers:** Daniel Vassallo,
Twitter post, May 18, 2020, 1:18 a.m., https://twitter.com/dvassallo
/status/ 1262251147135340544.

65 **their industry impact also expanded:** Jane Porter, "From Near
Failure to a $1.5 Billion Sale: The Epic Story of Lynda.com," *Fast
Company*, April 27, 2015, https://www.fastcompany.com/3045404
/from-near-failure-to-a-15-billion-sale-the-epic-story-of-lyndacom.

65 **Noxgear manufactures:** Elizabeth Kyle, "Dayton Startup Profile:
High Visibility Vest Makes International Impact," *Dayton Business
Journal*, November 5, 2019, https://www.bizjournals.com/dayton
/news/2019/11/05/dayton-startup-profile-high-visibility-vest
-makes.html.

66 **The idea of building:** Peter Fritz, interview with Justin Mitchell, *Office Anywhere*, podcast audio, April 13, 2020, https://peterfritz.co
/voice-messaging-beats-slack-zoom-yac-justin-mitchell.

67 **"Want to find a good":** Adam Wathan, Twitter post, May 14, 2020,
8:38 a.m., https://twitter.com/adamwathan/status/12609122515669
85223.

70 **"quantum of utility":** John Gruber, "A Quantum of Utility," *Daring
Fireball* (blog), n.d., https://daringfireball.net/linked/2009/04/02
/utility-paul-graham.

76 **"Over Thanksgiving break":** Lenny Rachitsky, "How the Biggest
Consumer Apps Got Their First 1,000 Users—Issue 25," *Lenny's
Newsletter*, May 12, 2020, https://www.lennyrachitsky.com/p/how
-the-biggest-consumer-apps-got.

CHAPTER 4: SELL TO YOUR FIRST HUNDRED CUSTOMERS

90 **"people will jump":** Dan Ariely, *Predictably Irrational: The Hidden
Forces That Shape Our Addictions* (New York: HarperCollins, 2008),
Kindle ed.

90 **This model, popularized by:** "The Freemium Business Model," AVC,
https://avc.com/2006/03/the_freemium_bu/.

92 **"Millions of people":** "Bring Your Creative Project to Life," Kickstarter.com, https://www.kickstarter.com/learn.

93 **products geared toward personal development:** "About Please-Notes," PleaseNotes.com, https://pleasenotes.com/pages/about.

93 **a PleaseNotes journal:** Ande Lyons, interview with Cheryl Sutherland, *Startup Life with Ande Lyons*, podcast audio, February 15, 2018, https://andelyons.com/use-creativity-clear-vision-confidence-rapid-results/.

93 **She eventually raised:** "PleaseNotes—Find Your Passion and Live It!," Kickstarter.com, December 18, 2019, https://www.kickstarter.com/projects/pleasenotes/pleasenotes-find-your-passion-and-live-it.

97 **Richest Self-Made Women:** Kerry A Dolan, Chase Peterson-Withorn, and Jennifer Wang, eds., "America's Richest Self-Made Women 2020," *Forbes*, October 13, 2020, https://www.forbes.com/self-made-women/.

97 **started out with cold calls:** Megan DiTrolio, "Stitch Fix's Katrina Lake Dishes Out Savvy Business Advice," *Marie Claire*, May 14, 2020, https://www.marieclaire.com/career-advice/a32376163/stitch-fix-katrina-lake-business-advice/.

97 **"The more shameless":** Sarah Spellings, "How I Get It Done: Stitch Fix CEO Katrina Lake," *The Cut*, December 30, 2019, https://www.thecut.com/2019/12/how-i-get-it-done-stitch-fix-ceo-katrina-lake.html.

99 **they found that working:** "Our Story," Mailchimp, https://mailchimp.com/about/.

99 **Chestnut and Kurzius have:** Jake Chessum, "Want Proof That Patience Pays Off? Ask the Founders of This 17-Year-Old $525 Million Email Empire," *Inc.*, December 11, 2017, https://www.inc.com/magazine/201802/mailchimp-company-of-the-year-2017.html.

102 **she decided to make one herself:** Jaime Schmidt, *Supermaker: Crafting Business on Your Own Terms* (San Francisco: Chronicle Prism, 2020), 24.

102 **She experimented for months:** Schmidt, *Supermaker*, 38.

102 **She set up a simple website:** Schmidt, *Supermaker*, 38.

102 **she found a rhythm:** Schmidt, *Supermaker*, 41–43.

103 **many times, they returned:** Schmidt, *Supermaker*, 53.

103 **"Early customer feedback":** Schmidt, *Supermaker*, 57.

CHAPTER 5: MARKET BY BEING YOU

107 **"Marketing is really":** Peter Economy, "11 Michael Hyatt Quotes to Inspire You to Happiness and Success," *Inc.*, February 11, 2016, https://www.inc.com/peter-economy/11-michael-hyatt -quotes-to-inspire-you-to-happiness-and-success.html#:~:text=% 22Marketing%20is%20really%20just%20about,others%20some thing%20you%20care%20about.

121 **launched its first podcast:** Ari Levy, "'Startup' Podcast Offers a Rare Fly-on-Wall View of Tech M&A After Gimlet's $200 Million Sale to Spotify," CNBC, October 22, 2019, cnbc.com/2019/10/22/startup -podcast-offers-inside-view-of-tech-ma-after-sale-to-spotify.html.

122 **If content is king:** Bill Gates, "Content is King," Bill Gates' Web Site, January 3, 1996, http://web.archive.org/web/20010126005200 /http:/www.microsoft.com/billgates/columns/1996essay /essay960103.asp.

123 **"Entrepreneurship: work 60 hours a week":** Sahil Lavingia, Twitter post, February 10, 2021, 8:08 p.m., https://twitter.com/shl/status /1359670684675239936.

131 **The COVID-19 pandemic accelerated:** Ali Mogharabi, "Digital Ad Spending Poised for Exceptional Growth," Morningstar, December 11, 2020, https://www.morningstar.com/articles/1014195/digital-ad -spending-poised-for-exceptional-growth.

CHAPTER 6: GROW YOURSELF AND YOUR BUSINESS MINDFULLY

139 **"Life is like riding a bicycle":** Albert Einstein, letter to his son Edu- ard (February 5, 1930), quoted in Walter Isaacson, *Einstein: His Life and Universe* (New York: Simon & Schuster, 2007), 367.

143 **"default alive or default dead":** Paul Graham, "Default Alive or De- fault Dead?," PaulGraham.com, October 2015, http://www.paulgra ham.com/aord.html.

147 **"digital by default"**: Tobi Lutke, Twitter post, May 21, 2020, 10:55 a.m., https://twitter.com/tobi/status/1263483496087064579.

147 **even giants like:** Jack Kelly, "Here Are the Companies Leading the Work-from-Home Revolution," *Forbes*, May 26, 2020, https://www .forbes.com/sites/jackkelly/2020/05/24/the-work-from-home -revolution-is-quickly-gaining-momentum/.

147 **"very excited to see"**: Sam Altman, Twitter post, May 21, 2020, 1:56 p.m., https://twitter.com/sama/status/1263529191581954049.

149 **"I thought we were just"**: Charlie Keegan, "Stitching Life into Hamilton," 41 Action News, KSHB-TV, Kansas City, MO, June 14, 2019.

152 **"A Kids Book About did"**: Megan Rose Dickey, "The Journey of a Kids Book Startup That Tackles Topics like Racism, Cancer and Divorce," *TechCrunch*, August 18, 2020, https://techcrunch.com /2020/08/18/the-journey-of-a-kids-book-startup-that-tackles -topics-like-racism-cancer-and-divorce/.

157 **one founder departs the company:** Steli Efti, "The Secret to Successful and Lasting Co-Founder Relationships," *The Close Sales Blog*, December 23, 2020, https://blog.close.com/the-secret -to-successful-and-lasting-co-founder-relationships/.

158 **four types of communication styles:** Ellie Lisitsa, "The Four Horsemen: Criticism, Contempt, Defensiveness, & Stonewalling," *The Gottman Relationship Blog*, April 23, 2013, https:// gottman.com /blog/the-four-horsemen-recognizing-criticism-contempt-de fensiveness-and-stonewalling/.

CHAPTER 7: BUILD THE HOUSE YOU WANT TO LIVE IN

165 **"You can dream"**: Jeff James, "Leadership Lessons from Walt Disney—How to Inspire Your Team," *Disney Institute Blog*, https:// www.disneyinstitute.com/blog/leadership-lessons-from-walt -disney--how-to/.

167 **"What's the one thing"**: Gary Keller and Jay Papasan, *The One Thing: The Surprisingly Simple Truth Behind Extraordinary Results* (London: John Murray, 2019).

171 **"celebrate every opportunity to learn"**: Wildbit.com, https://wildbit .com/story/philosophy.

178 **WeWork is one example:** Charles Duhigg, "How Venture Capitalists Are Deforming Capitalism," *New Yorker*, November 23, 2020, https://www.newyorker.com/magazine/2020/11/30/how-venture-capitalists-are-deforming-capitalism.

178 **"the tendency in most":** Laurence J. Peter and Raymond Hull, *The Peter Principle: Why Things Always Go Wrong* (New York: Bantam, 1970).

187 **"$115k–$135k/year":** Adam Wathan, Twitter post, May 24, 2020, 3:32 p.m., https://twitter.com/adamwathan/status/1264640396640 096264.

CHAPTER 8: WHERE DO WE GO FROM HERE?

191 **"We are born to wander":** Robert Moor, *On Trails: An Exploration* (New York: Simon & Schuster, 2017).

194 **"A healthy man wants":** "Confucius," http://web-profile.net/articles /quotes/confucius.

195 **"dizziness of freedom":** Søren Kierkegaard, *The Concept of Anxiety: A Simple Psychologically Oriented Deliberation in View of the Dogmatic Problem of Hereditary Sin*, translated by Alastair Hannay (New York: Liveright Publishing Corporation, 2015 [originally published 1844]).

196 **"time billionaire":** Tim Ferriss, interview with Graham Duncan, *The Tim Ferriss Show*, March 1, 2019, https://tim.blog/2019/03/01/the -tim-ferriss-show-transcripts-graham-duncan-362/.

199 **"Occasionally I angel invest in":** Sahil Lavingia, Twitter post, June 1, 2020, 11:00 a.m., https://twitter.com/shl/status/12674711265 71057158.

202 **In 2019, Shopify:** "We Need to Talk About Carbon," Shopify, September 12, 2019, https://news.shopify.com/we-need-to-talk-about -carbon.

202 **By 2030, Google:** *24/7 by 2030: Realizing a Carbon-Free Future*, Google white paper, September 2020, available at www.gstatic.com /gumdrop/sustainability/247-carbon-free-energy.pdf.

INDEX

q